For Folake

Sylvia Anderson

Advance Praise for

# EXECUTIVE PRESENCE

## THE MISSING LINK BETWEEN MERIT AND SUCCESS

"With clarity and honesty, Sylvia Ann Hewlett shines a light on a central truth: if we fail to master the 'intangibles' of leadership we're in danger of missing the mark. Sylvia's impeccable research and guidance prepares us to crack the Executive Presence code."

> —Ann Beynon, commissioner, UK Equality and Human Rights Commission; director for Wales, BT

"This is a powerful and urgent book for young professionals climbing the ladder. Credentials alone will not get you the next big opportunity. You also need Executive Presence—the ability to signal confidence and credibility. In this immensely readable study, replete with vivid stories as well as hard data, Sylvia Ann Hewlett tells us how to ace EP."

> —Sallie Krawcheck, business leader, 85 Broads

"Sylvia Ann Hewlett has taken some of the mystery out of the claim that 'you just don't have what it takes' in this groundbreaking book on Executive Presence. Combining story after story with well-grounded research, this book provides a simple guide that will help you crack the code to career success."

> —Katherine W. Phillips, Paul Calello Professor of Leadership and Ethics, Columbia Business School

"Whether you are an aspiring corporate star or a seasoned veteran, Sylvia Ann Hewlett's *Executive Presence* will captivate you—pithily written, laden with stories, and grounded in the latest research. You will find a lesson that you can't wait to adopt on every page. It is the modern handbook on the art of visible leadership for which many of us have been waiting."

> —Trevor Phillips, former chairman, UK Equality and Human Rights Commission

E

**EXECUTIVE PRESENCE**

P

THE MISSING LINK BETWEEN MERIT AND SUCCESS

# EXECUTIVE PRESENCE

## SYLVIA ANN HEWLETT

HarperCollins books may be purchased for educational, business, or sales promotional use. For information, please e-mail the Special Markets Department at SPsales@harpercollins.com.

FIRST EDITION

*Designed by William Ruoto*

Library of Congress Cataloging-in-Publication Data has been applied for.

ISBN: 978-0-06-2246899

15  16  17  18   OV/RRD   10  9  8

*To the band of heroes who made this research possible:*

*Barbara Adachi, Antoine Andrews, Cynthia Bowman, Daina Chiu, Jennifer Christie, Deborah Elam, Anne Erni, Gail Fierstein, Anne Fulenwider, Michelle Gadsden-Williams, Trevor Gandy, Heide Gardner, Rosalind Hudnell, Fran Laserson, Janice Little, Carolyn Buck Luce, Tom Morrison, Nisha Rao, Eileen Taylor, Geri Thomas, Karyn Twaronite, Anré Williams, Melinda Wolfe, and Tony Wright.*

# ACKNOWLEDGMENTS

This book is close to my heart, and it gives me particular pleasure to acknowledge the extensive help I've received from family and colleagues.

First and foremost I'd like to thank my husband, Richard Weinert, and our children, Shira, Lisa, David, Adam, and Emma. Their enthusiasm and support has lightened my load during the months I've spent focused on this book. I'm immensely appreciative.

I owe a huge debt of gratitude to Melinda Marshall. Her deep knowledge of this subject matter and stellar writing skills contributed enormously to this book. I am extremely grateful to her.

My senior team—Peggy Shiller, Lauren Leader-Chivée, Laura Sherbin, Tai Green, and Karen Sumberg—has also been extraordinary. In particular, Peggy's management prowess and Laura's quantitative skills were critical in helping me meet the ambitious deadlines of this fast-track book. I thank them both.

I'm also enormously grateful to the senior executives (and their companies) who underwrote and helped shape the survey research that underpins this book: Jennifer Christie and Anré Williams (American Express), Cynthia Bowman and Geri Thomas (Bank of America), Anne Erni and Melinda Wolfe (Bloomberg), Trevor Gandy (Chubb), Michelle Gadsden-Williams (Crédit

# Acknowledgments

Suisse), Barbara Adachi and Tom Morrison (Deloitte), Nisha Rao and Eileen Taylor (Deutsche Bank), Karyn Twaronite (EY), Antoine Andrews (Gap Inc.), Deborah Elam (GE), Gail Fierstein (Goldman Sachs), Rosalind Hudnell (Intel), Heide Gardner and Tony Wright (Interpublic Group and Lowe and Partners), Anne Fulenwider (*Marie Claire*), Daina Chiu and Janice Little (McKesson), Fran Laserson (Moody's Foundation). Their generous support has gone well beyond funding. Over the past two years these corporate leaders provided precious access and lent wise counsel. A big thank-you.

The co-chairs of the Task Force for Talent Innovation contributed key insights and thought leadership. I would like to thank Caroline Carr, Anthony Carter, Erika D'Egidio, Valerie Grillo, Patricia Fili-Krushel, Cassandra Frangos, Sandy Hoffman, Annalisa Jenkins, Patricia Langer, Leena Nair, Lisa Garcia Quiroz, Craig Robinson, Lucy Sorrentini, and Elana Weinstein— for their belief in the importance of this study, and their ongoing dedication to the mission of our organization.

A special word of appreciation to Jonathan Burnham and Hollis Heimbouch of HarperCollins. Their commitment to this project was critical to getting the book off the ground. I'm also indebted to Molly Friedrich, who encouraged me to transform dense research into much more narrative-driven prose. Her advice was spot on. In addition, I want to thank my daughter Lisa Weinert and Fiona McMorrough for their contributions to the communication strategy that underpins this book.

A word of thanks to DeAnne Aguirre, D'Army Bailey, James Charrington, Suzi Digby, Brady Dougan, Bob Dudley, Kent Gardiner, Judith Harrison, Mellody Hobson, Linda Huber, Sallie Krawcheck, Laura Lopata, Carolyn Buck Luce, Debbie Maples, Tim Melville-Ross, Harold Morrison, Kerrie Peraino, Katherine Phillips, Trevor Phillips, Ripa Rashid, Jane Shaw, Keisha Smith,

# Acknowledgments

Debora Spar, Mark Stephanz, Joe Stringer, Joel Tealer, Tiger Tyagarajan, Richard Weinert, and Cornel West—and to all the women and men who took part in focus groups, interviews, and Insights In-Depth sessions.

I'm deeply appreciative of the research support and editorial talents of the CTI team: Michael Abrams, Noni Allwood, Joseph Cervone, Terri Chung, Fabiola Dieudonné, Colin Elliott, Courtney Emerson, Christina Fargnoli, Mark Fernandez, Catherine Fredman, Tara Gonsalves, Lawrence Jones, Anne Mathews, Andrea Turner Moffitt, Birgit Neu, Nicholas Sanders, Sandra Scharf, Roopa Unnikrishan, and Jennifer Zephirin. I also want to thank Bill McCready, Stefan Subias, and the team at Knowledge Networks, who fielded the survey and were an invaluable resource throughout the course of the data collection.

Last but not least, a heartfelt thank-you to the members of the Task Force for Talent Innovation for providing cutting-edge ideas and impressive amounts of collaborative energy: Elaine Aarons, Rohini Anand, Redia Anderson, Renee Anderson, Diane Ashley, Nadine Augusta, Terri Austin, Ann Beynon, Anne Bodnar, Kristen Bruner, Kenneth Charles, Tanya Clemons, Joel Cohen, Nicola Davidson, Whitney Delich, Jill DeSimone, Nancy Di Dia, Mike Dunford, Vanessa Edwards, Lance Emery, Traci Entel, Nicole Erb, Titus Erker, Grace Figueredo, Trevor Gandy, Lisa George, Tina Gilbert, Tim Goodell, Kathy Hannan, Kara Helander, Ginger Hildebrand, Alex Hiller, Kate Hoepfner-Karle, Celia Pohani Huber, Sharon Jacobs, Nia Joynson-Romanzina, Eman Khalifa, Inci Korkmaz, Kelly Knight, Denice Kronau, Janina Kugel, Yolanda Londono, Margaret Luciano-Williams, Lori Massad, Donna-Marie Maxfield, Ana Duarte McCarthy, Beth McCormick, Mark McLane, Piyush Mehta, Sylvester Mendoza, Carmen Middleton, Erica Nemser, Pamela Norley, Mark Palmer-Edgecumbe,

# Acknowledgments

Pamela Paul, Sherryann Plesse, Monica Poindexter, Susan Reid, Jennifer Rickard, Karin Risi, Eiry Roberts, Dwight Robinson, Jacqueline Rolf, Jennifer Silva, Debbie Storey, Lynn Utter, Cassy Van Dyke, Vera Vitels, Lynn O'Connor Vos, Jo Weiss, Meryl Zausner, and Fatemeh Ziai.

# CONTENTS

# Contents

My first run-in with executive presence (EP) occurred when I was seventeen. I was in the second year of the sixth form and applying for the ultimate "reach" schools—Oxford and Cambridge. I'd gotten a certain distance, having passed the rigorous entrance examinations, but was now facing a round of interviews. I anticipated a rough time. I knew enough about the world to understand that I came from the "wrong" background (Welsh, working-class), and my knees knocked and I broke out in a cold sweat at the mere thought of facing the scrutiny of Oxbridge dons. I feared they would size me up and decide I did not have "it," which of course they had in spades.

Seeing my distress and eager to be helpful, my mum volunteered to "dress" me for my first interview at St. Anne's College, Oxford. She'd read a ton of Nancy Mitford novels and thought she knew what kind of clothes the "upper crust" wore. I didn't push back—I knew I was clueless. I'd grown up in a backwater mining community and had few clothes and no social graces. I was eager for help. Having battled huge odds to pass the entrance tests, I knew that only this interview stood between me and a coveted place at one of the most distinguished universities in Europe. And I had a good shot—half of those interviewed got a place. I just had to figure out how to look the part of someone who moved in the right circles.

# Prologue

So early one December morning we hit the winter clearance sales—rising at the crack of dawn so that we would be at the head of the herd storming C&A (a department store in Cardiff). And did we score! In the sales racks of the ladies' suits department my mum found exactly what she was looking for: a nubby tweed suit with a fox collar. And I don't mean the collar was made out of fox fur. I mean the collar was a fox—or most of a fox. The tail was a big feature (you were supposed to fling it around your neck as extra protection against the winter cold), and there were beady eyes and two sets of claws.

As might be expected, my Oxford interview was a disaster. The admissions committee was gobsmacked. I literally took their breath away. They simply did not know what to make of a seventeen-year-old who wore a fox and seemed to be trying to look like the Queen Mother—especially since this particular seventeen-year-old spoke English with a thick working-class Welsh accent (more on that in chapter 3). I did not get in . . . and was devastated. But it was hard to blame my mum, she had tried so hard.

To my great relief I got a second shot at my dream. A month later I learned that I'd also passed the Cambridge entrance examinations (in those days the two top universities crafted their own rigorous tests). I was invited to go for an interview. I told my mother that she was off the case—this time I was dressing myself. Remembering "the look" of the other female candidates at Oxford, I borrowed a pleated skirt and a simple sweater from a friend and ironed my unruly hair so it fell in the shining sheets that seemed to be in vogue. Despite an acute attack of nerves, I did well enough in the interview. Three weeks later I learned that I had won a place. I was over the moon. I knew that a Cambridge education would transform my life prospects.

Looking back, I realize that I didn't need to do brilliantly

in those interviews. I merely needed not to stick out like a sore thumb. The fact is, in the 1970s, Oxford and Cambridge universities, under pressure from the British government, were trying hard to diversify and had committed to increasing the number of female and working-class individuals in the student body. Unbeknownst to me, I was a prime candidate, and those admissions committees were leaning over backward to give me a place. But the fox collar *and* the Welsh accent were just too much for class-conscious Oxbridge dons. I just stuck in their craw. Losing the fox was a winning idea.

Given the travails of Oxbridge entrance, you would have thought I had learned a thing or two about the power of appearance. Perhaps I did, but it was hard to hang on to. Time and time again I made costly mistakes.

Take my hippie professor phase. My first job was in academia, and when I joined the Barnard College faculty as assistant professor of economics, I assumed that since I was working on a college campus, and not on Wall Street, it was okay to be young and fun. So I wore my hair waist-long and I specialized in flowing ethnic skirts—my favorite was hand-stitched and had a rather loud patchwork quilt pattern. I failed to understand that looking as though I was on my way to Woodstock got in the way of establishing authority on the job. Given my age—I was twenty-seven when I started this job—it was a stretch to convince anyone I was a professor and not just another student. The last thing I needed was to compound the challenges I faced as the youngest faculty member—and one of the few females in the economics department. I now understand that my early struggles to command attention and respect in lecture halls and faculty meetings did not center on content or delivery (I was a clear, crisp speaker and knew my material cold), but rather centered on the way I presented myself.

The good news is that I eventually fixed the way I looked, evolving a signature style that combined elegance and professionalism with a "safe" amount of idiosyncratic flair (more on this in chapter 4). But I wasn't out of the woods on the EP front. Twenty years later I hit another—and much more serious—image problem. It turns out that EP is a fragile thing: It needs to be nurtured, invested in, and curated. I failed to do this and fell flat on my face—necessitating an EP makeover.

Here is what happened.

In 2002, Tina Brown (who, at that point, headed up Talk Miramax Books) published my book, *Creating a Life*. It launched on April 7, 2002. The weekend before, *Time* magazine ran a cover story on the book and the CBS News show *60 Minutes* aired a feature. These stories triggered a maelstrom of media attention. The *New York Times* and *BusinessWeek* did feature pieces on the book; so did *People* and *Parade* magazines. I appeared on the *Today* show as well as on *Oprah* and *The View*. The coup de grâce: In late April I was lampooned on *Saturday Night Live*, confirming the fact that my book had briefly entered the zeitgeist.

Alas, the good news did not last.

On May 20 I picked up the *New York Times* and glimpsed on the front page a noisy headline blaring "The Talk of the Book World Still Can't Sell." Halfway through the first sentence my blood ran cold—the subject of the article was *my* book. In gleeful tones the reporter, Warren St. John (a young hotshot business writer), walked the reader through how *Creating a Life* was shaping up to be a total bust on the sales front. He found the explanation all too simple: "Women are just not interested in shelling out $22 for a load of depressing news about their biological clock," he opined smugly and snarkily. I was stunned. These dismissive words did not describe the book I had written.

I didn't even need to finish the article to understand the dam-

age it would do—which was swift and devastating. In a matter of weeks, *Creating a Life* was DOA—and, figuratively speaking, so was I. I went from being a much-feted author to a pariah, since one of the many problems of being trashed on the front page of the *New York Times* is that everyone is in the know. It's like being stripped in public. My entire circle of friends and colleagues read this piece. In fact, one reason I felt so bad was that I knew that many more people would read the alpha-male spin of Warren St. John on page A1 of the *New York Times* than would ever read *Creating a Life*. That article effectively buried what was my most deeply felt and painstaking book.

I tried to rebound, of course. Over that summer I threw myself into a new book project. In early September I met with Molly Friedrich, my longtime literary agent, to pitch it. "I'm thinking something more fine-grained, more academic," I offered. Looking me in the eye, Molly let me have it. "Sylvia," she said, "there's not going to be a next book. Given your recent track record, you're not going to get a decent publisher or a decent advance. You need to get a day job."

I was stunned. How had this happened? How could my livelihood be in jeopardy and my reputation—carefully built over years—be in tatters? The explanation dawned painfully and slowly: I had constructed, but hadn't curated, my personal brand. I'd invested in it—establishing myself in both academia and public policy circles as an intellectual heavyweight with the chops to take on the really thorny questions of our time—but I hadn't proactively protected it. I might have realized, when the *Time* story broke, that I was seriously out of my depth. Although I'd written critically acclaimed books before (*When the Bough Breaks* won me a Robert F. Kennedy Book Award), it didn't occur to me to arm myself with a PR professional, someone who could craft a media campaign that would amplify, rather than distort, my message. In-

stead I reveled in the immediate impact of *Creating a Life* and had plunged in with naïve delight, doing every radio show and print interview that came my way. Quite quickly the content of the book was dumbed down, making me vulnerable to attack. It's one thing to be thoughtfully critiqued by the *New York Review of Books*, quite another to be bent out of shape by the *National Enquirer.*

So, having squandered my hard-won gravitas, I had little choice but to start over, building my credibility and authority brick by heavy brick. As a woman north of fifty, I did not have time on my side. But decades spent doing good work in both academia and the public sector had given me a network and sponsors that I could turn to for a fresh start. That fall I applied for, and got, two adjunct teaching positions—one at Columbia and one at Princeton. I poured immense energy into these roles and by the spring was able to convert the Columbia position into a continuing part-time job—as director of the Gender and Policy Program at the School of International and Public Affairs. With my brand refurbished, I found I had fresh currency in the very circles I wanted to court: professional women and their employers. Because, of course, I hadn't changed my focus: I still wanted to make a difference, to transform women's lives and their career prospects. This time around I decided to focus on changing the face of leadership, to help create the conditions that empower many more women (and other previously excluded groups) to sit at decision-making tables. In 2004 I founded a think tank (the Center for Talent Innovation) which has become an influential global organization and done much to accelerate the progress of women and minorities around the world. In driving this tranche of work I've written four books and eleven articles—all for the Harvard Business Review Press. I've learned my lesson. Nowadays I proactively curate where I publish and avoid the popular media. I want to be seen as an intellectual heavyweight, not Typhoid Mary.

My bumpy journey on the EP front has contributed special energy as well as important perspectives to this book. To flag some of the more significant:

Appearance challenges are not trivial, but they do tend to be easily fixed and pale in comparison to other, more profound EP problems. Remember that fox collar? Although it blew my chances at St. Anne's College, I was able to quickly ditch that look and improve my chances when I got a second shot.

Reputational glitches are much more serious—and immensely difficult to recover from. Resurrecting my brand after the disastrous launch of *Creating a Life* took about six years. I didn't breathe easy until my body of new work had spawned a fifth *Harvard Business Review* article. At that point I knew I had reestablished my gravitas.

The irony, of course, is that this entire discussion centers on image, not substance. Whether we're talking about appearance or gravitas, we're focusing on what we're signaling to the world rather than what we're really accomplishing. What kind of outfit I wore to my Oxford interview had no bearing on my intelligence or my preparedness for an Oxford education. Seen from that vantage point, it should not have mattered. But it did. Enormously. Similarly, the fact that *Creating a Life* was dragged into the gutter by the popular press (and talk radio) had no bearing on the intrinsic value of this book. After all, it made it onto the *BusinessWeek* list of the ten most important books of 2002 and I still meet women whose lives were transformed by its content. But messaging matters. Enormously. The wrong message and the wrong messenger can destroy careers whatever the substantive reality.

So read this book. Understanding EP and cracking its code will do wonders for your ability to achieve success and do what you want with your life.

# E
EXECUTIVE PRESENCE
# P

# 1

President Obama has it. So does Facebook's chief operating officer, Sheryl Sandberg. It's embodied by people as varied as Jamaican sprinter Usain Bolt, the late British prime minister Margaret Thatcher, celebrated Burmese parliamentarian Aung San Suu Kyi, and actress Angelina Jolie, especially since she made public her courageous decision to tackle her heritage of breast cancer. Nelson Mandela exuded it—when he donned the Springboks' jersey and shook the hand of the captain of the winning all-white national rugby team the world knew that South Africa had found a leader intent on reconciliation.

*It* is executive presence—and no man or woman attains a top job, lands an extraordinary deal, or develops a significant following without this heady combination of confidence, poise, and authenticity that convinces the rest of us we're in the presence of someone who's the real deal. It's an amalgam of qualities that telegraphs that you are in charge or deserve to be.

And here I want to underscore the word *telegraph*. Executive presence is not a measure of performance: whether, indeed, you hit the numbers, attain the ratings, or actually have a transformative idea. Rather, it's a measure of image: whether you signal to others that you have what it takes, that you're star material. If you're able to crack the EP code you'll be first in line for the next

plum assignment and be given a chance of doing something extraordinary with your life.

The amazing thing about EP is that it's a precondition for success whether you're a cellist, a salesperson, or a Wall Street banker.

Every October, a distinguished jury assembles at Merkin Concert Hall in New York City to judge the finalists in the Concert Artists Guild's international competition. Several weeks of rigorous auditions have already taken place, and an applicant pool of 350 instrumentalists and singers from all over the world has been whittled down to 12 extraordinary young musicians. Last fall, I attended the final auditions.

A twenty-three-year-old Korean violinist had the first slot in the program.[1] He entered the auditorium from stage left and after taking a detour behind the Steinway piano, sidled onto the apron of the stage looking painfully ill at ease. Head bowed, he stared at the floor, doing his best to avoid eye contact with the jurors as he waited for his accompanist to get settled. Unfortunately, it took a while, since she had trouble adjusting the piano stool to the right height. The violinist shifted his weight awkwardly from side to side. I could feel the restlessness rising in the audience. One juror blew his nose; another started tapping her foot.

Finally the accompanist struck the first chords of a glorious—and immensely difficult—Beethoven sonata, and the violinist raised his instrument and started playing. But it took a while for the audience to be drawn in—to give him a chance.

An Irish mezzo-soprano had slot number two. The energy was very different from the get-go. She walked confidently onto the stage, shoulders squared, head held high. Her dress was perfectly chosen, a simple navy blue sheath that conveyed elegance and seriousness of purpose. I spent a moment silently applauding her choice, but my attention was quickly drawn to her face, which

was adorned with a radiant, joyous smile. She seemed to be telling me that something immensely pleasurable and exciting was about to begin. The jury caught the vibe and leaned forward in anticipation, lips parted, wanting and expecting to be impressed.

The other finalist who stood out was number seven—a twenty-year-old cellist who had just received an extraordinary review for a recording she'd done of the Dvorak cello concerto. As she started playing, I sensed trouble. It was her arms. They flapped. Every time she tackled her cello with a vigorous downbow, the flesh bounced up and down. I was mesmerized—and so were the jurors. The problem was not excessive weight (she was of medium build) but her choice of clothing. Her dress was a disaster—a black silk number with a skimpy, ill-fitting halter top. No wonder her arms flapped—anyone's would in such a getup.

My heart went out to this young musician. A distracted jury is never a good idea. Throughout her twenty-minute program the judges failed to focus their full attention on her music, and her powerful playing did not get its due.

These are the finalists that stand out in my memory: Musicians number one and seven did not receive prizes. The mezzo-soprano did.

I've gone to these auditions several times over the years and what always impresses me are the number of seemingly peripheral factors that feed into the judging process. For sure, each finalist in this international competition clears a high bar of excellence. All of the young musicians I heard at Merkin Hall last fall were enormously skilled. They wouldn't have gotten through the early rounds of the competition if they weren't outstanding practitioners of their musical craft.

But in the finals what distinguished one from another was all of the nonmusic stuff. The way they walked onto the stage, the cut of their clothes, the set of their shoulders, the spark in

their eyes, and the emotion that played on their faces. All of these things established a mood either of tedium and awkwardness or of excited anticipation.

Richard Weinert, president of the Concert Artists Guild, marvels at the importance of nonmusical factors. "As we've grappled with launching the careers of these extraordinarily talented artists, we've learned that how they present themselves matters enormously. Yet oftentimes they don't see it as being part of what they need to do. Graduates of the top conservatories—Juilliard, Curtis, and the like—have had little training in it and haven't given it much thought. It often comes as a shock when we explain that how they move and what they wear onstage—how they establish rapport with the audience—is as important as their musical skills."

A recent study underscores the importance of image (or EP, to use the language of this book) in the world of music. In a piece published in the *Proceedings of the National Academy of Sciences*, University of London researcher Chia-Jung Tsay, working with a sample audience of one thousand, reports that people shown silent videos of pianists performing in international competitions picked out the winners more often than those who could also hear the sound track.[2] The study concludes that the best predictor of success on the competition circuit was whether a pianist could communicate passion through body language and facial expression.

This evidence from the world of music underscores the tremendous power of image: How musicians present themselves creates an indelible impression. We might like to think that we're evaluating a performance of Bach or Shostakovich based solely on what we hear, but in reality we're profoundly conditioned by the visuals. Judgments are made before the first note sounds in the concert hall.

It's no different in the workplace.

## CRACKING THE EP CODE

So how do we figure out this image thing?

One financial sector CEO told me in an interview, "I can't describe it, but I sure know it when I see it." The fact is, many of us find EP a woolly and elusive concept. We can't define it, and we have a hard time putting our arms around it.

Which is why I wrote this book.

Two years ago, my research team at the Center for Talent Innovation set out to crack the code, fielding a national survey that involved nearly 4,000 college-educated professionals—including 268 senior executives—to find out what coworkers and bosses look for when they evaluate an employee's EP. In addition to this survey research, we also conducted forty focus groups and interviewed a large number of leaders.

We learned that EP rests on three pillars:

- How you act (gravitas)
- How you speak (communication)
- How you look (appearance)

While the specifics vary depending on context (what works on Wall Street doesn't necessarily work in Silicon Valley), these three pillars of EP are universal. They are also somewhat interactive. For example, if your communication skills ensure you can "command a room," your gravitas grows exponentially; conversely, if your presentation is rambling and your manner timid, your gravitas suffers a blow.

One thing to note at the start is that these pillars are not equally important—not by a long shot. Gravitas is the core characteristic. Some 67 percent of the 268 senior executives we surveyed said

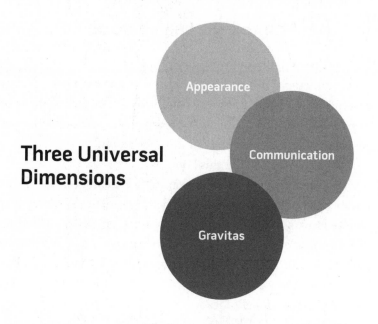

**Three Universal Dimensions**

**Figure 1. EP: Three universal dimensions**

that gravitas is what really matters. Signaling that "you know your stuff cold," that you can go "six questions deep" in your domains of knowledge, is more salient than either communication (which got 28 percent of the senior executive vote) or appearance (which got a mere 5 percent).

Projecting intellectual horsepower underpins gravitas, but there's more to this attribute than being the smartest gal or guy in the room. It's about signaling that you have not only depth and heft but also the confidence and credibility to get your point across and create buy-in when the going gets rough—when your enterprise or venture is under extreme pressure. In fact, projecting confidence and "grace under fire" was the number-one pick of senior executives asked to identify what constitutes EP.

Ten years ago, another trait might have been the top pick. In the years immediately before the 2008 global recession CEOs were treated like demigods—rock stars in wing-tipped shoes—and charisma was a much-sought-after attribute. A huge personality and forceful presence marked a person as a leader. Think of GE's Jack Welch or Virgin's Richard Branson. But in the wake of the financial crisis, the ability to appear calm, confident, and steady in the face of an economic storm is far more important.

How do people know you have gravitas? You *communicate* the authority of a leader—through your speaking skills and ability to command a room. Indeed these two communications traits are the top picks (one and two) of the senior executives in our survey. Your tone of voice, bearing, and body language can also add to—or detract from—your ability to hold your audience's attention, whether you're presenting to a small team or addressing a plenary session of a large conference.

One surprise finding of our research is that, when it comes to communication, eye contact matters enormously. Being able to look your coworkers in the eye when making a presentation, or being able to make eye contact with the audience when making a speech, has a transformative effect—on your ability to connect, to inspire, to create buy-in. This fact has serious consequences. It means that you need to lose your glasses, your notes (and oftentimes your PowerPoint), and just wing it. This is not easy. It requires a huge commitment of time since you need to prepare and practice so thoroughly that the arc of your remarks becomes part of your muscle memory. There are no shortcuts.

In our survey senior executives told us that appearance is inconsequential—only 5 percent identified it as the most important aspect of EP. This is deceptive. The fact is, appearance (as we saw in the musical competition) is a critical first filter. While senior execs (and coworkers) see it as unimportant in the long run,

it constitutes an initial hurdle. If a young female associate turns up at a client meeting wearing a tight blouse and a miniskirt, she may not be invited back—no matter how impressive her qualifications or how well prepared she is. The fact is, blunders on the appearance front can get you into serious trouble—and get you knocked off the list of those in contention for stretch roles or plum assignments—no matter how brilliant you are. It's sobering to understand how quickly this happens. As we shall see in chapter 2, research conducted by Harvard Medical School and Massachusetts General Hospital suggests that colleagues size up your competence, likability, and trustworthiness in 250 milliseconds—based simply on your appearance.

The only good news in our data on appearance is that "grooming and polish" was chosen by more respondents than "physical attractiveness" or "body type" (whether you are slim or well-endowed, tall or short) as a key contributor to EP. The comfort here of course is that grooming and polish can be learned and acquired. It's a huge relief to know that cracking the code on the appearance front isn't a function of what you were born with; rather, it's a function of what you do with what you've got.

Part one of this book (chapters 2, 3, and 4) lays out the key components of gravitas, communication, and appearance. It tells us what our bosses and coworkers are looking for and gives us the wherewithal to deliver it. Part two describes some pitfalls and trip wires, because it's not a simple matter, this cracking of the code. Most complicated of all is the fundamental tension between conformity and authenticity. How much should you fit in? How much should you stand out? How much of the "real you" are you prepared to sacrifice on the altar of success?

While every professional we interviewed told us he or she wrestles with this tension, the struggle is particularly painful for women and minorities. For these historically underrepresented

groups are dealing with a double whammy. Not only do they need to shape and mold their identities to fit an organizational culture (something everyone faces), but they're required to "pass" as straight white men. Why? Because this continues to be the dominant leadership model. Eighty-eight percent of those who sit in corner offices on Wall Street and Main Street look this way.

One comforting piece of news here is that with time, the authenticity struggle gets easier. With age and experience, those who truly do have the right stuff on the gravitas front earn the right to be more authentic, to bring more of themselves to work.

Michelle Gadsden-Williams, a senior executive at Credit Suisse, recalls the moment when she realized that the ways in which she was different did not constitute the bar keeping her from moving up, but rather the lever that might propel her progress. Early on in her career as a young manager in a global pharmaceutical firm, she dared deliver to the executive committee an unwelcome verdict: Among black employees, attrition was high and morale low because these individuals struggled against subtle bias in the organizational culture. When the CEO, genuinely mystified, asked why, Gadsden-Williams described three instances of bias she had personally experienced at the firm, and then suggested some solutions. Walking out of the room that day, she says, she was filled with anxiety: Had she stepped over the line? Would her outspokenness cost her? But on the contrary, the courage she exhibited brought her leadership potential into sharper focus for the firm's executive committee. Not only were her recommendations adopted, but Gadsden-Williams was promptly promoted.

When it comes to bringing one's full self to work, no one inhabits their authenticity better than my friend Cornel West, professor of philosophy at Union Theological Seminary and civil-rights crusader. With his distinctive Afro, black three-piece

suits, and fearsome oratory, West never fails to make a powerful and lasting impression. Yet as the first-ever African-American to graduate from Princeton with a Ph.D. in philosophy, and one of the first African-Americans to win admission to Harvard as an undergraduate, he has endured more than his presence today belies. West is well acquainted with the soul-crushing pressure to conform to the expectations of people quite unlike himself in order to win their confidence, trust, and support. I know something, myself, of just how daunting it is to win acceptance at an Ivy League institution where you don't look, sound, or act like those on the committee making the appointment decisions. But it was precisely the crucible of his circumstances that revealed, for West, the imperative of touting rather than hiding his unique strengths. Today, his keen insight, born of empathy, into the unmet needs of "the 99 percent"; his fire-and-brimstone delivery style; and his formal attire exude gravitas and garner him the attention of everyone from President Obama to Oxford dons.

So take heart: While cracking the EP code can be onerous and sometimes eats into your soul, this work and these struggles allow you to flower and flourish. Once you've demonstrated that you know how to stand with the crowd, you get to strut your stuff and stand apart. It turns out that becoming a leader and doing something amazing with your life hinge on what makes you different, not on what makes you the same as everyone else.

# 2

In May 2010, as a torrent of crude oil spewed from the ocean floor into Gulf of Mexico waters, ABC News anchor Jake Tapper drilled into Bob Dudley, then BP's managing director, for an explanation.

"So 'topkill' failed," Tapper opened, referring to BP's attempt to plug the well by pumping heavyweight drilling mud into it. "Should the American people prepare themselves for an uncomfortable fact—that this hole will not be plugged until August, at the earliest?"[3]

Dudley—features composed, collar unbuttoned—affirmed that, while August was a possibility, BP was working around the clock and would contain the spill as soon as was humanly possible.

Tapper turned up the heat. "As you know there are serious questions as to whether or not there have been corners cut—safety corners—that resulted in this accident," he said. Why, for instance, did BP use "the risky option" of a metal casing known to buckle under high pressure?

Dudley calmly countered that no corners had been cut, no risky options pursued.

"But why were operations not shut down immediately until well control could be restored?" Tapper persisted, his tone ever more accusatory.

"That is another issue the investigation is going to look at

very, very carefully," Dudley responded evenly, never breaking eye contact with the camera lens. He then went on to say that getting to the bottom of this tragedy was BP's top priority. The company owed that to the people of the Gulf.

Two months later, Dudley again sat in the hot seat—this time, on *PBS NewsHour*, where he answered questions put to him by hard-hitting host Ray Suarez about the catastrophic consequences of the spill.[4] Dudley, his voice steady but charged with empathy, stepped in with his first response. "I've seen the devastation," he began. "I went down to Grand Isle two weeks ago and I saw the oil on the beaches. . . . I traveled out to Grand Pass and saw the oil in the marshes and talked to the local people." He then leaned forward and looked Suarez in the eye. "You know," he said, "we're going to make good on the claims from individuals and businesses down there." And he methodically laid out the steps BP was taking to do just that. Suarez then made a reference to the *Exxon Valdez* incident—a very badly handled oil spill. Dudley didn't shy away from the implied comparison; instead he explained that BP wouldn't "hide" behind a declaration of bankruptcy or some legal processes, as Exxon had done. Suarez continued to press, but during the entire grilling there wasn't a single question Dudley avoided or refused to answer and he came over as a compassionate, considered, and competent leader, and that indeed is his image.

Bob Dudley, these days CEO of BP, is not a leader who gets hot under the collar, but it's not because he's stayed out of the kitchen. On the contrary, as he detailed in an interview with me, his career in Big Oil, which began at Amoco at the height of the OPEC crisis, has put him at the epicenter of the industry's worst nightmares. As CEO of TNK-BP, he battled a group of Russian oligarchs intent on squeezing him out. He dealt with various kinds of harassment, including, some say, threats to his life, and, when his visa was denied, proceeded to run the company from

an undisclosed remote location. Fresh from that challenging set of experiences, he was put in charge of BP's operations in Asia and the Americas, reporting to CEO Tony Hayward. Then the Deepwater Horizon exploded, Hayward imploded (more on that later), and BP stock tumbled to half its value. In July, the firm tapped Dudley, who was heading up the Gulf Coast Restoration Organization, to take over from Hayward. Such was Dudley's credibility that before the well was even capped, BP's share price took an upturn.

When I attempted during our interview to credit him with BP's recovery, Dudley demurred with characteristic humility. "There were a lot of people who performed unbelievably well," he said. But nothing, he agreed, is more important in troubled times than a leader who projects calm and confidence. "I want people around me who can be clear-thinking and calm in a crisis," he emphasized. "I don't believe I've ever been able to judge or trust a person unless I can see what they're like under fire."

Early in her career as an academic, Katherine Phillips emerged as the voice at the table courageous enough to point out the elephant in the room. In only her second year on the faculty at Northwestern's Kellogg School of Management, Phillips told her colleagues at a succession-planning meeting that it was "a waste of energy" to discuss replacing Max Bazerman, a world-renowned faculty member who'd recently left, because none of them was willing to allocate the necessary resources to lure in an equally towering intellect.

"You guys have already taken his office, his courses, and his grant monies and divvied them up among yourselves," she pointed out, referring to the fact that Bazerman's empire had already been picked over. "What's left? What are you willing to give back? X, y, or z? No one top-notch will consider coming to Kellogg

without an amazing package that needs to include x, y, and z." She let that sink in, then added, "Let's not waste time talking about it anymore, because what I'm seeing is, Max has already been replaced"—she raised an index finger and jabbed it—"by you . . . and you . . . and you."

"Well, they were stunned," Phillips told me, marveling at her own youthful bravado. "But after the meeting two senior faculty members thanked me for saying what I did. And it sparked a much more honest discussion in the department."

This incident established Phillips as someone others could count on to speak the truth when no one else dared. She is today the Paul Calello Professor of Leadership and Ethics at Columbia Business School—the first African-American woman to hold a chair at this prestigious school. "You could say that 'speaking truth to power' has become part of my personal brand," she observes. "I've never been afraid to say what others won't—and people have come to count on me for that."

In 2012, a newly appointed CEO of a medical device manufacturer faced a difficult watershed moment. Recently enacted U.S. healthcare rules meant the firm would be hit with a 2.3 percent excise tax—an unforecasted loss equivalent to $75–$100 million in reduced profits. This new leader knew he needed to move quickly and cut expenses across the board—including (most painfully) head count. By strategically reallocating resources from poorly performing units to more promising divisions, he could probably save hundreds of jobs. Still, there would be layoffs. More than two hundred, in fact.

The CEO delivered the bad news himself. "I pulled the group together, stood in front of them, and walked them through why the company needed to make these cuts and answered their questions," he told me in an interview. "Obviously I couldn't get rid of

their pain—and I didn't try to. But I did want them to know that it wasn't a personal thing (these were hardworking, loyal employees) but a structural thing (the company needed to downsize in order to survive and thrive going forward). I also wanted them to know that there would be a 'package' and we would do our utmost to help them find a way forward." He paused. "Still, it was a pretty tough two hours. They were surprised and distressed, and felt blindsided—even betrayed. They let me know it in no uncertain terms. But one thing was clear to me. I needed to be there. I wasn't about to hide in my office and expect a junior colleague to deal with the tough stuff."

Lots of leaders do precisely that, I pointed out. Had he seen *Up in the Air*, where George Clooney plays the professional ax man, flying around the country doing the dirty work for leaders lacking the courage to fire employees themselves? He had.

"You have to be there in bad times as well as good, to show you lead from the heart as well as from the head," this CEO observed. "This emotional intelligence thing is important. If you don't reach out personally, if you don't show empathy, if you don't speak from your heart, you lose the trust and respect of not only your employees but also your investors. And then you're truly powerless."

## THE RIGHT STUFF

We all know a real leader when we see one. Like Bob Dudley, he or she projects an aura of calm and competence that instills faith even in—*especially* in—the white-hot center of a crisis. Like Kathy Phillips, he or she reveals integrity and demonstrates courage by uttering truths when they are inconvenient or most unwelcome. And like our medical-device firm CEO, he or she demonstrates

courage and emotional intelligence that secures followership even in the wake of news that would seemingly destroy it.

These qualities connote gravitas, that weightiness or heft that marks you as worth following into the fire. Gravitas is the very essence of EP. Without it, you simply won't be perceived as a leader, no matter what your title or level of authority, no matter how well you dress or speak. Gravitas, according to 62 percent of the leaders we surveyed, is what signals to the world you're made of the right stuff and can be entrusted with serious responsibility.

But what is it, really? What makes up gravitas—this elusive but all-important piece of executive presence? How do you come by it, and how might you telegraph it?

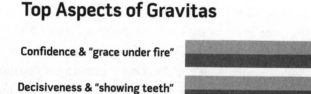

**According to Senior Leaders**
# Top Aspects of Gravitas

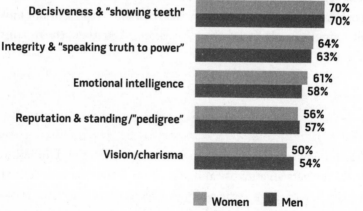

Figure 2. Top aspects of gravitas

CTI research reveals gravitas to consist of six key behaviors and traits.

What strikes me about this list is how entirely contemporary it is. It makes perfect sense, in our troubled times, that senior leaders in our survey—and virtually all of the CEOs I interviewed—prize "grace under fire" (79 percent concur it's critical for women's EP, and 76 percent concur it's critical for men's EP). Just consider what we've been through in the past ten or fifteen years in terms of unprecedented events. The century opened with a bang: not Y2K, but the bursting of the dot-com bubble, wiping out billions. In 2001, the unthinkable occurred with the September 11 terrorist attacks, driving us to war in both Afghanistan and, by 2003, Iraq.[5] Before the year 2001 was out, the economy took another major blow when it was revealed that accounting fraud and corporate complicity had bankrupted Enron, the $100 billion energy and commodities firm. Six months later, telecommunications titan WorldCom revealed a similar scandal on an even more spectacular scale, stiffing creditors to the tune of $5.7 billion. This was only a taste of the defrauding to come: The subprime mortgage crisis in 2008 robbed Americans of their jobs and savings, triggering a recession in the United States and touching off a global financial meltdown from which much of Europe has yet to recover. Every day, it seems, we're rocked by news of ever more scandalous behaviors by those entrusted with our financial security, whether it's the $891 million in customer accounts that MF Global misappropriated to cover trading losses in 2011 or the 2012 revelations that British banks had colluded to fix LIBOR.

Is it any wonder, given this spate of scandals, that we're drawn to leaders who keep their promises, keep their cool, and show compassion as well as courage in making the truly hard choices?

Gravitas alone won't secure you the corner office, of course: You've got to have the skill sets, the experience, and the innate

talent to qualify for the job. As Linda Huber, chief financial officer at Moody's, observes, "Substance must be the bedrock in order for someone to be taken seriously." But if you have that depth of experience and those vital skills, gravitas is all that's between you and that top job. It can't be faked, but it can be cultivated.

## GRACE UNDER FIRE

How do you come by composure in a crisis?

You've got to reach inside yourself to that place where you believe, you absolutely *know*, you're eminently qualified to do the job at hand.

"Self-confidence is your iron core," says Anne Erni, head of human resources at Bloomberg LP. "To lean into the wind when your heart is pounding, you have to believe in yourself, deep down. It's not something you can fake."

Steeliness is forged, history shows us, in the crucible of crisis—and it may take a crisis for you to discover your core of confidence. Angela Merkel, Germany's chancellor since 2005, may not solve the euro crisis, but no one contests her competency or credibility as a leader, in large part because she never loses her composure. Christine Lagarde, head of the International Monetary Fund and prior to taking over that institution, France's finance minister, likewise enjoys universal respect for her poise and levelheadedness in steering her country through the straits of the 2008 liquidity crunch. Margaret Thatcher, Britain's former prime minister, will forever be known as the Iron Lady for having weathered, with nary a hair out of place, protracted crises at home (double-digit unemployment, a national coal miners' strike), a lingering cold war with the Soviets, and a Falkland Islands showdown with Argentina. Most of us are like teabags,

to borrow from Eleanor Roosevelt's shrewd words: We don't know how strong we are until we're in hot water.

That you may have boiled the water in which you steep doesn't necessarily undermine your opportunity to acquire gravitas. Look at recent headline makers who've proven their mettle not by averting mistakes, but by owning up to them. For example, Jamie Dimon, CEO of JPMorgan Chase, failed to forestall some $5.8 billion in trading losses in 2011—which is not much of a testament to his leadership prowess! Dragged before Congress to explain why, he might well have joined the infamous ranks of dissemblers like WorldCom chief Bernard Ebbers. But instead, Dimon accepted responsibility and equably answered questions, maintaining his composure and exuding confidence without coming off as arrogant. Far from gutting his gravitas, the public flogging actually seemed to bolster it. Jack Welch, the former CEO of General Electric, observed in *Fortune* that Dimon would be remembered as a man who "dusted himself off, got back on his horse and rode on—stronger and a whole lot wiser."[6] Investors in JPMorgan actually cheered his performance, according to Money. com. History may yet judge Dimon a scalawag, but even his detractors came away impressed by his grace under fire.

So while avoiding catastrophe may demonstrate competence, it is handling catastrophe that confers gravitas. Recall Captain Chesley "Sully" Sullenberger, the US Airways pilot who landed in the Hudson River after striking a flock of Canada geese. Avoiding the geese was not an option; what *was* an option for this leader was not succumbing to the "worst sickening, pit-of-your-stomach falling-through-the-floor" feeling he suffered moments before the crash.[7] As a result of Sully's extraordinary poise and control, every passenger and crew member survived that forced landing unharmed.

You will make mistakes. You will suffer the mistakes of others.

Accidents completely out of your control will befall you. Each of these represents, however, a monumental opportunity to acquire and exude gravitas: to reach within yourself, at the height of the storm, for that eye of calm, and to speak and act from that place of clarity. Because when you demonstrate that your confidence cannot be shaken, you inspire confidence in others. At worst, you'll win their forgiveness and forbearance. Very possibly, you'll win their trust and loyalty.

Tim Melville-Ross tells of just such a watershed moment in his career, when a mistake he made might have cost him his job, his career, and his reputation—but instead provided him occasion to man up and show the public what he was really made of. Back when he was CEO of Nationwide, the United Kingdom's biggest building society (equivalent to a savings and loan in the United States), Melville-Ross acceded to pressure from one of his top directors to adopt a questionable business practice, one that would help the firm hold its margins in a shrinking economy. "To my undying shame, we tried to screw the customer," he admits. "A good building society simply doesn't do that. I made the wrong decision." But then he made the right one: He sacked that director and made a very public apology. He wrote a letter to the London *Times*, one that he closed by inviting readers to write to him personally. Many did write, Melville-Ross told me, and took him to task for his blunder. The larger result of his falling on his sword, however, was restored faith in Nationwide—and, interestingly, in him personally. "It established me as a leader of integrity," he says, "a reputation which has carried me through many a storm since." Melville-Ross is today chair of the Higher Education Funding Council for England and president of the Institute of Business Ethics.

You have this same choice. In a crisis, you can lean into the wind, acknowledge your shortcomings, and rise above them; or

you can take cover. You can acquire gravitas, the cornerstone of a real leader. Or you can demonstrate that, no matter what your actual title, you really don't deserve to be in charge.

Just look at Tony Hayward. When the BP oil spill first made the news, Hayward seemed to have the public's trust because he'd shown himself to be "frightfully" candid about BP's previous stumbles and "dreadful" performance. But the minute he attempted to distance himself and the company from blame—the infamous "What the hell did we do to deserve this?" comment to BP executives, and then, two weeks later, observing to the *Guardian* that "the amount of volume of oil and dispersant we are putting into [the Gulf] is tiny in relation to the total water volume"—the public turned on him.[8] His comments were seen as conveying arrogance rather than confidence. Any chance he may have had to restore public opinion—by apologizing, for instance—he squandered with ever more stunning displays of insensitivity, the most memorable being his infamous remark "I'd like my life back."[9] These petulant words provoked a savage reaction. News commentators couldn't believe that he was complaining about his schedule—missing a few summer weekends seemed a paltry sacrifice in the context of this catastrophic spill that had wreaked havoc in the Gulf. So many residents had lost their livelihoods—and eleven oil rig workers lost their lives. So instead of calming the waters, Tony set fire to them. It was a blunder that cost him his job.

## SHOWING TEETH

Lynn Utter, who is today chief operating officer of Knoll Inc., a global leader in furniture and textile manufacturing, recalls the moment in her career when she first showed teeth. She'd just been

named head of the container unit at Coors Brewing Company, replacing a thirty-year company veteran to become the company's first female senior leader. Just a few months into the role, Utter sat in a meeting with half a dozen male board members who were debating whether to invest millions of dollars to fund a start-up as part of a joint venture. Having done her homework, she was utterly clear on how and why Coors should do the deal. Still, she listened to others, hoping for insights outside her own, until finally, fed up with the equivocation, she stood and addressed the room. "If we do not invest," she said with calm, sturdy authority, "we are not living up to the fundamental philosophy of our partnership. If we do nothing, in fact, the entity is doomed. Either we step up, or we call it off."

Under her leadership, the investment went forward. "I do not think they expected me to have that kind of backbone," Utter says. "But I'd done my homework and knew the numbers cold. I knew what we needed to do and felt it was up to me to show strength and point the way forward."

Making difficult decisions is what we look to leaders to do. It is not so much about rendering the right decision, but about rendering a decision at a time when no one else dares, that confers gravitas, because it telegraphs that you have the courage, as well as the confidence, to impose a direction and take responsibility for it. Yahoo CEO Marissa Mayer showed she had the chops when she announced that all employees, starting in June 2013, would need to be working out of Yahoo's offices.[10] For the survival of the company, whose share price was tanking, she was revoking telecommuting privileges. "Speed and quality are often sacrificed when we work from home," read the memo that employees received from HR head Jackie Reses. "We need to be one Yahoo!, and that starts with physically being together."[11] The move sparked a firestorm: Some leaders (Jack Welch among them) applauded

the move as an appropriate piece of discipline for the ailing firm; others (Richard Branson was one) condemned it as "a backwards step."[12] But Mayer had the courage to recognize that business as usual was not going to bootstrap Yahoo out of its death spiral. She made a bold, if unpopular, decision. She showed teeth. That display of confidence and courage boosted her gravitas and, consequently, her shareholders' faith in her ability to turn the tide.

CTI research finds that 70 percent of leaders consider decisiveness to be a component of EP for both men and women, second only to confidence in a crisis, making it a core aspect of gravitas. Being able to make decisions isn't so much the issue as needing to appear decisive in public—the difference, again, between doing the job of a leader and *looking* like one as you're doing it, between demonstrating competence and exuding *presence*. George W. Bush clearly recognized this imperative when he zeroed in on being "the Decider" and built this as a central part of his brand. Mitt Romney similarly trumpeted his assertiveness on the presidential campaign trail; in his view leadership and "showing teeth" were synonymous. Better to get a reputation, as president, for being a hard-ass than a wuss—"soft" on terrorists, or illegal immigrants, or dictators.

Given that showing teeth draws on so many stereotypically male attributes—aggression, assertiveness, toughness, dominance—it's ostensibly easier for males to appear decisive. Yet if the emergence of testosterone clinics is any indication, men aren't necessarily naturals at showing teeth. The *Financial Times* reported that, in search of "the positive side of aggression," men are dosing up on testosterone, convinced the hormone will confer the "alpha male personality" of a bona fide Wall Street mover and shaker.[13] One clinic, located steps away from the New York Stock Exchange,[14] offers twice-weekly treatments as part of a $1,000-and-up monthly regimen.[15] The injections aren't without

risk: Side effects include sleep apnea, increased risk of heart disease, growth of latent tumors, and testicular shrinkage.[16] But the results, to hear the clinic's Wall Street clientele describe them, more than justify the risks. Testosterone makes them feel bolder, louder, and more assertive, they say; as a result, they're more comfortable showing teeth and taking risks. "It's important to project an aura of invincibility," one trader confided to me. The way he sees it, he's buying job security—no small thing in an industry that's shed one hundred thousand jobs since 2008.

Women, however, definitely have a harder row to hoe—not in *being* decisive, it bears repeating, but in *appearing* to be. Women like Marissa Mayer who render decisions that demand action risk being perceived as "unfeminine"—aka unlikable—in the eyes of their peers and subordinates, a phenomenon we'll explore at much greater length in chapter 6. It's the classic double bind: If you're tough, you're a bitch and no one wants to work for you, but if you're not tough, you're not perceived as leadership material and you won't be given anyone to work for you. It's a high-wire act that every capable woman has had to perform, and the higher she goes, the more perilous the act. A senior colleague and mentor of a female tax attorney whose meteoric rise to CFO at Lehman Brothers garnered her intense scrutiny recounted to me some of the advice he felt obliged to give the attorney as she navigated her way to the C-suite. "She had no problem finding her voice at the table with fourteen other men," he told me. "But that was the problem: She was very demanding, very assertive. And that was no way to impress these guys, many of whom had spent fifteen, twenty years at the firm." He counseled her to "damp it down," to be more sensitive to the other voices. "You walked in and spoke like you are the next chairman of the firm," he remembers telling her. "You may be, and it may be a good goal for you . . . but you can't act like that today. You have to be a little more sensitive to the senior men sitting around the table with you, or they'll eat you alive."

Male or female, the way to walk the line between decisive and difficult may be, as Lynn Utter demonstrates, to dish it out very discriminately—to hide your teeth more often than you bare them. Real leaders don't issue edicts just to look and sound like they're in charge. Real leaders listen, gather critical information, weigh the options carefully, look for a timely opening (typically when everyone else is writhing in indecision), and *then* demand action.

"Oftentimes it is just as important to know when being decisive is *not* the thing to do—to let events play out in a certain way and bide your time," cautions Bob Dudley. "I see a lot of people trying to be too decisive too quickly."

When the moment demands a decision that you're prepared to render, step forth and render it. Just choose those moments with care.

## SPEAKING TRUTH TO POWER

In the aftermath of Superstorm Sandy, Governor Chris Christie of New Jersey shocked his fellow Republicans by publicly heaping praise on Barack Obama just days before the 2012 presidential election. Speaking live on Fox News, with images of the ravaged state playing over the airwaves, Christie told viewers that he'd had three conversations in the last twenty-four hours with the president, asking that his state be declared a federal disaster to expedite funds, and that that morning Obama had signed the paperwork. "I have to give the president great credit," Christie concluded. "He's been very attentive and anything I've asked for, he's gotten to me. He's done, as far as I'm concerned, a great job for New Jersey." When asked if he'd be touring the state later by helicopter with Governor Romney, Christie, a vocal supporter of the Republican candidate just days before, told the correspon-

dents he didn't know and wasn't interested. "If you think right now I give a damn about presidential politics," he said heatedly, "then you don't know me."[17]

Those who know Christie weren't, in fact, shocked by his behavior. Mike DuHaime, an advisor to the governor, observed he was acting true to form. "He calls 'em as he sees 'em," he told the *New York Times*.[18] That's what Christie does: When homeowners refused to evacuate from New Jersey's barrier islands, Christie called them "both selfish and stupid."[19] Prior to Sandy, he called President Obama "the most ill-prepared person to assume the presidency in my lifetime."[20]

Christie doesn't hesitate, that is, to speak his truth—however impolitic it may be, however mighty the audience he offends with it. And that candor marks him, paradoxically, as a presidential contender.

Speaking truth to power, as more than 60 percent of our respondents affirm, is a potent affirmation of leaderlike courage. The higher you go in an organization, the more impressive you are when you demonstrate you have the spine to share your convictions. "I want people who will walk into my office and say, 'Here's where I differ, I want to talk to you about it,'" affirms Tiger Tyagarajan, CEO of Genpact. "I love that! This is the kind of courage I'm looking for, in addition to the given of stellar performance."

Make sure, however, that when you challenge authority, you're coming from a core of unshakable values. Anything less and your actions will be perceived as insubordination and/or arrogance—the opposites of gravitas.

And then prepare to be truly tested.

Financial powerhouse Sallie Krawcheck established early on in her career a penchant for telling it like it is. As a research analyst on Wall Street, she downgraded Travelers for its acquisition of bro-

kerage firm Salomon Brothers, a move that earned her the fury of Citicorp's Sandy Weill (Citicorp would acquire Travelers to form Citigroup). Impressed with her intellectual integrity as well as her analysis skills, however, Weill eventually hired her to head up Citigroup's Smith Barney unit, promoting her within two years to be CFO of Citigroup. Krawcheck continued to tell it like it was, suggesting, at the height of the 2008 financial crisis, that the company partially refund its clients for investments positioned by Citi as low risk that had taken a nosedive during the downturn. CEO Vikram Pandit wasn't appreciative of this piece of advice and fired her.

The story doesn't end there. In 2011, the integrity and courage Krawcheck exhibited at Citi won her the top job at Merrill Lynch, which had recently been taken over by Bank of America. Her brief: to make this much-revered wealth management house profitable again. Despite huge success on this front (revenues rose by 54 percent in her second quarter on the job), she found herself in the crosshairs of new CEO Brian Moynihan, whose leadership had resulted in losses of $8.8 billion across Bank of America during that same quarter.[21] By September of that year, Krawcheck was out.

"I've found that speaking truth has not always stood me in good stead in terms of my career progression," Krawcheck told me when we discussed her extraordinary journey. "But it always, always, always stood me in good stead in terms of managing businesses." She added, with heartfelt pride, "Had I to do it over again, I wouldn't do it any differently. Not one thing."

## DEMONSTRATING EMOTIONAL INTELLIGENCE

Mitt Romney's compulsion to show teeth—to remind us at every turn that his tough leadership style had made him a phenomenally

successful CEO—might have garnered him more votes in the run-up to the 2012 presidential election had he not, at the same time, demonstrated at every turn his utter insensitivity toward half the electorate. Like Tony Hayward, Romney was tone-deaf when it came to tuning his remarks for constituencies outside his war room. Comments such as noting that his wife had "a couple of Cadillacs" didn't persuade voters of his love for American cars, but rather that he lived in a rich man's bubble and was insulated from working people's reality. In a similar vein, his comment that he had consulted "binders full of women" to fill his cabinet as governor served to underscore how out of touch he was with the sensibilities of working women. The final blow, delivered at a private fund-raiser and captured on video that quickly went viral on the Web, was his sweeping condemnation of 47 percent of the electorate as freeloaders who pay no income tax! (Freeloaders, it turned out, included not-yet-employed returning veterans and the disabled.)

Romney's 47 percent comment "did real damage" to his campaign, as he himself conceded, underscoring just how important emotional intelligence—or EQ, as psychologist Daniel Goleman calls it—has become what we look for in leaders.[22] A hefty majority of our respondents see EQ as very important, with 61 percent noting its importance for women's executive presence, and 58 percent noting its importance for men's. And here's why: While decisiveness and toughness in a leader signal conviction, courage, and resolve, when untempered by empathy or compassion these same characteristics come off as egotism, arrogance, and insensitivity.

Look at Marissa Mayer's decision to force Yahoo's staff to return to their desks on campus. Issuing this edict showed teeth, as we've discussed, but regrettably, it also showed a leader out of touch with the realities other working parents contend with. Mayer drew fire not for being tough but for being hypocritical,

having solved her own child-care issues by building a separate cubicle next to her office for her infant son and nanny. "I wonder what would happen if my wife brought our kids and nanny to work and set 'em up in the cube next door?" joked the husband of one Yahoo mom.[23] His voice was tinged with bitterness.

Making and enforcing unpopular decisions is indeed part of showing you've got the chops to be put in charge. It's just that in today's ever-flatter organizations, acting insensitively actually compromises your ability to create buy-in among employees and realize optimal outcomes for the firm. This was the conclusion two researchers from Harvard and Stanford reached after spending weeks on two offshore oil rigs studying the culture change that management had initiated to improve safety and performance. The research team expected that, in this most dangerous and macho of work environments, aggression, bravado, and toughness not only would be on display but would be embraced and rewarded. But as a result of management's stated goals—bringing down work-site injuries and bringing up capacity—they witnessed a remarkable shift in attitudes and behaviors among the crews on oil rigs. Workers confirmed that, previously, the culture discouraged asking for help, admitting mistakes, or building community. The crew, in prior years, had been "like a pack of lions," with the guy in charge being the one who could "basically out-perform and out-shout and out-intimidate all the others." Once the emphasis shifted to safety, however, the company stopped rewarding "the biggest baddest roughnecks" in favor of men who could admit to mistakes, seek help when they needed it, and look out for each other. Over a period of fifteen years, this shift in values and norms helped the oil company achieve its goals: The accident rate fell by 84 percent and production hit an all-time high.[24]

Even on an oil rig, that is, demonstrating emotional intelligence (EQ) is a key leader trait because it builds trust—essential in con-

ditions where bravado could get you killed and a lack of concern for the team might cause others to wonder if you were cutting corners and compromising their safety. In less life-threatening conditions, however, EQ is just as important for building trust because demonstrating it shows you have not only self-awareness but also situational awareness. It's absolutely vital in white-collar worlds such as finance, law, and medicine to show you're capable of reading a situation, and the people in it, correctly. Standout leaders who can be trusted to pick up on all relevant cues win the trust of followers to steer them through an uncertain future.

Our interviewees spoke of the importance of EQ in particular in "reading a room"—the room being a metaphor for your immediate audience, in person or virtual. *What's the vibe, or unarticulated emotion you need to address or temper? What do people need from you in order to move forward?* Leaders who pick up on these cues know when to be decisive and when to hold back; when to show teeth, and when to retract their claws. "It may be more important to comfort a room than command it," points out Kent A. Gardiner, chairman of international law firm Crowell & Moring LLP, "because at times it can further consensus-building and problem-solving." Gardiner, whose career has encompassed RICO prosecutions and major civil and criminal antitrust litigation, describes how he cooled one particularly heated mediation session. "Everybody was unhappy, everybody was antagonistic, so getting up and pounding away was only going to increase the gulf," he says. "I let a little venting occur, and then I got up and said, 'Let's think about it this way,' very much respecting the other side's position, but then trying to move us all beyond a litigation resolution toward a business resolution. And people listened. People felt like it was a discussion, not just a fight."

It's not simply managing your own feelings, although restraint

on that front, as Gardiner shows, makes an enormous difference. Rather, it's recognizing and acting in accord with the feelings of others.

"Not showing that you have an understanding for people's feelings is absolutely a no-no," says the CEO of the medical device firm. "It does not negate your ability to be tough and make tough decisions, or tell people when things are not going right or when they are not doing their jobs. You can do all of that with compassion."

Most important, you can acquire this sensitivity. EQ isn't an inborn intelligence so much as a muscle you build through experience. Recall Michelle Obama's misstep in 2010 when she whisked her daughter and some forty friends off to Spain for a glitzy summer vacation. It was something Jackie O might have been celebrated for, but then, Jackie's husband hadn't gotten voted into office to fix a global financial crisis. To be spending lavishly on a European holiday when her fellow Americans were grappling with unemployment, protracted recession, and gutted retirement plans was a Romneyesque blunder, one that got her dubbed "a modern-day Marie Antoinette."[25] That was the last time the first lady acted so heedlessly; indeed, over the last several years Michelle Obama has acquired perfect pitch. For example, when Hadiya Pendleton, a fifteen-year-old honor student who'd performed at the 2012 inauguration, was killed in a random shooting just a week later, Michelle attended her funeral and met with her family. In April she returned to Chicago to meet with other high schoolers terrorized by gang shootings and make an impassioned plea for tighter gun control laws nationwide. No one who saw her deliver that speech could doubt the first lady felt our pain.[26] The gaffes of her first years in the White House have been forgotten.

## RIGHT-SIZING YOUR REPUTATION

Make no mistake: Your reputation does precede you, either bestowing gravitas or bleeding you of it. Before you enter a room or open your mouth, your reputation speaks for you—never more so than today, when word of your latest blunder or scandal races at lightning speed around the globe in 140 characters or less. People will have formed an opinion of you before you're in a position to help them form it, which is why 56 percent of leaders concur that reputation matters a great deal in establishing EP for women and 57 percent agree it matters for men. Managing your personal brand is almost a job unto itself, lest it be managed for you by people who don't hold your best interests at heart. You've got to be proactive in asserting who you are, what you stand for, and how you'd like to be perceived.

Even in Hollywood, where celebrities are fixated on honing their image, Angelina Jolie's brand is viewed as a towering accomplishment. She's clearly a standout beauty and accomplished actress, but she's also a universally admired public figure with depth, heft, and clout. How did this happen? First off, she's distinguished herself among movie stars by her dedication to underprivileged children the world over, several of whom she's adopted. Her efforts seem to come from a deep place, and far exceed the photo-op moments that characterize celebrity "involvement" in good causes. After filming *Lara Croft: Tomb Raider* in Cambodia, she started traveling with UNHCR, the United Nations' refugee agency, as a goodwill ambassador, a commitment that's taken her on forty-some field missions since 2001 and won her, in 2012, a special envoy appointment. She started the Maddox Jolie-Pitt Foundation to address conservation in Cambodia and the National Centre for Refugee and Immigrant Children to provide

free legal aid to young asylum seekers, work that earned her membership on the Council on Foreign Relations.[27] She does much of this work off the radar of the press, and yet the gravitas it has conferred is palpable.

Many a sterling reputation is forged in the crucible of scandal. Recall Magic Johnson, the all-star basketball player who contracted HIV/AIDS. When news of his illness broke in 1991, AIDS was a scourge associated with homosexuality and intravenous drug use. Johnson made a courageous choice: He made himself very publicly an example of the consequences of unprotected sexual activity, transforming the behavior of homosexuals and heterosexuals alike, and curbing the spread of AIDS as a result. Johnson's reputation as a basketball legend regained its luster, and today he's known as a former megastar, but also as a successful businessman, author, and philanthropist extraordinaire.

Bear in mind that your reputation is not a function simply of your deeds and actions: Social media and the ubiquity of smartphones—with their handy dandy cameras—conspire to make your reputation a function of what people see, including your attire, office décor, automobile, vacation home, and collectibles. This visibility makes it imperative you style your environment as carefully as you style yourself—a point we'll take up at length in chapter 4, on appearance. Even the photos on your desk or office wall say something about you, so make sure they communicate a message that's in keeping with your mission. One chief financial officer at a tech giant in Silicon Valley learned this the hard way: She featured on her office wall a photograph taken of herself emerging from a limo clad in a very short black dress that revealed a stunning length of well-toned thigh. The image, which had appeared in a national glossy magazine, had accompanied an article trumpeting her rapid ascendance in an almost exclusively male culture—a triumph she felt warranted further exposure on

her wall. But her colleagues felt otherwise. One of them insisted she take it down. "Is this what you want people to focus on? Is this your leading edge?" he asked her angrily. "It's critical to the success of this firm that shareholders feel confident in your judgment. Anyone seeing this photo would have to question it."

## VISION AND CHARISMA

If there's one name today that's synonymous with visionary leadership, it's Steve Jobs.

Jobs is also synonymous with innovation, but that's because every product to emerge from Apple during his tenure demonstrated his commitment to machines and environments so beautifully and flawlessly designed that they supported an intensely pleasurable user experience. And Jobs consistently deployed his design values, applying them to Apple hardware, Apple software, Apple stores, and online Apple platforms such as iTunes. Even in his attire—black turtleneck, perfectly fitting blue jeans—Jobs telegraphed the simplicity and elegance of his creations.

Jobs's means of achieving this vision secured him equal parts loathing and reverence, to hear his biographers tell it. A perfectionist incapable of compromise, he hounded his team to rework the first iPhone even as the launch deadline loomed. He deemed it too utilitarian, too masculine, too task-focused to seduce users into plunking down five hundred dollars for an untried product. The beauty of line and touch needed to be more obvious. He was as ruthless in paring down his teams as he was in paring away extraneous features on Apple products, arguing that "A" engineers were not only fifty times better to have than "C" engineers, but also that "A's do not like playing with C's."[28] Jobs's perfectionism and his impatience with people who didn't share his venera-

tion for design earned him a reputation as a control freak and an unfeeling boss. But because some of these very qualities aligned with Apple's brand—flawless function, minimalist design, and a seamless marriage of the two—these traits served, paradoxically, to make Jobs revered by colleagues and customers the world over. In the decade leading up to his untimely death in 2011, Jobs secured an almost cultlike following. When he died he was deeply mourned. There were candlelight vigils in Shanghai, São Paulo, and San Francisco, and the glass walls of the Apple Store around the corner from my New York apartment were festooned with handwritten Post-its. I read two of the notes: A fourteen-year-old thanked Jobs for the fun she had with her iPhone, it was so easy to use and made her feel cool; a twenty-nine-year-old father wanted Jobs to know about his undying gratitude—his iPad was transforming the life prospects of his three-year-old autistic son.

Exceedingly few of us will conjure up or drive a vision as powerfully as Jobs did. Yet to communicate gravitas, it's critical you telegraph vision. Fifty-four percent of the leaders we surveyed think "the vision thing" is key for men; 50 percent believe it matters a lot for women, too.

Joanna Coles, editor of *Cosmopolitan*, has long had a vision of spearheading a different kind of women's magazine, one that has its fair share of fashion and fun but also encourages women to use their new clout to make a difference in this world. She has always believed that such a magazine could be enormously commercially successful. She finally got a chance to realize her vision when, in 2007, she was appointed editor of *Marie Claire*—a fashion magazine that focuses on thirty-something-year-old professional women. During her five-year tenure she shifted its editorial content so as to include important pieces of investigative journalism that targeted women's issues. One of the first pieces she spearheaded was a story on women's rape kits getting tossed

to one side (shelved, filed, or just plain lost) instead of being tested and used in criminal prosecutions. This article proved riveting to readers—and drove circulation to a new high. It zeroed in on a young woman whose rapist was out there in the community raping other women because no one had bothered to log into a national database the DNA sample collected from her. But this piece, besides driving sales, also vaulted the magazine into a more serious realm, short-listing *Marie Claire* for a prestigious journalism award. With that success, Coles had license to embark on a socially conscious editorial agenda, one that helped shine a spotlight on women such as Angelina Jolie for their humanitarian achievements, and not just their fashion sense. Nowadays, she's bringing the same sensibilities to *Cosmopolitan*, inspiring a whole new generation of women to take themselves seriously. It hasn't always earned her praise or won her popularity trophies: Coles is hard-driving and famously demanding of her staff—there is a whiff of *The Devil Wears Prada* about her. But this doesn't concern her in the least. "I won't be one of those people who lies on her deathbed thinking, 'I wish I had spent less time in the office,'" she muses. "I will lie on my deathbed thinking, I wish I'd given everything one hundred and fifty percent instead of the occasional one hundred percent."

Indeed, as Mellody Hobson, president of Ariel Investments, points out, likability is what women loathe to sacrifice. Leadership cannot be a popularity contest, she affirms.

"There are people who absolutely don't like me," Hobson told me. "I make them uncomfortable. But I also know they respect me. I'm someone with whom they'd want to be in a foxhole. That's how we talk about leadership at this firm: *Who do you take into the foxhole?* You don't take people you like, you take someone who is going to save your life in a really bad situation. You don't want a whiner. You don't want someone who panics. And you certainly

don't want fake optimism," she elaborates. "You want brutal optimism. Great leaders are *brutally* optimistic."

## BLUNDERS

In focus groups and interviews we asked senior executives (and white-collar employees across the board), What are the mistakes? What gets you in trouble on the gravitas front? And how serious is this trouble? These were the top picks:

The blunders shown below trigger a wide range of consequences. While a star salesman can recover from such missteps as an offensive joke or a lack of depth on some technical issue, or a talented computer engineer can withstand accusations of

**Gravitas Blunders**
From focus groups and interviews

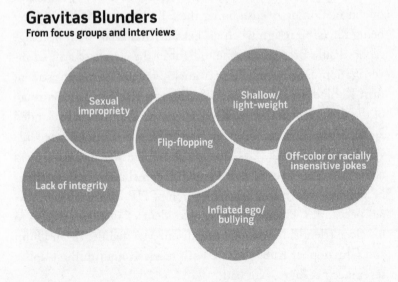

Figure 3. Gravitas blunders

bullying (as long as it's in the past tense), there are two blunders that are career killers. Lack of integrity (think Jon Corzine) and sexual impropriety call into question people's judgment and values on such a fundamental level that they completely lose their gravitas—and ability to lead.

Sexual impropriety takes some kind of prize as a career killer—at least for men. Recent headliners include former congressman Anthony Weiner, former International Monetary Fund chief Dominique Strauss-Kahn, former four-star general and CIA director David Petraeus, and former Hewlett-Packard CEO Mark Hurd. A quick Google search turns up a raft of other C-suite-ers who all recently became "formers" as a result of sexual shenanigans: CEO Brian Dunn of Best Buy, CEO Gary Friedman of Restoration Hardware, and CFO Christopher Kubasik of Lockheed Martin are among the recent crop.

Interestingly, while sexual impropriety can knock the powerful off the top perch, there's usually a chance at recovery or some sort of consolation prize cushioning the fall—for men, at least. After being forced to resign when his extramarital affair with his biographer Paula Broadwell came to light in the course of an FBI investigation, David Petraeus was quickly snapped up by investment firm Kohlberg Kravis Roberts & Company to become chairman of the firm's newly created KKR Global Institute. He also landed faculty positions at the City University of New York and the University of California, Los Angeles, where he was given a named chair. Mark Hurd engineered a similar comeback. Six weeks after he was shot down from the top perch of HP as a result of a sexual peccadillo, Hurd became co-president of Oracle—thanks to his close friendship with Larry Ellison. Meanwhile, Brian Dunn and Christopher Kubasik have both received multimillion-dollar severance packages. Not bad!

The women involved in these sexual peccadillos fare much

less well. One reason is that many of these relationships involve a senior male leader and a female subordinate who has neither the power nor the prestige to help her recover. For example, in the wake of her affair with Petraeus, Paula Broadwell was disciplined by the military and lost both her commission in the reserves and part of her retirement benefits. The female contractor who allegedly carried on that affair with Mark Hurd has not been able to find work since the scandal broke and is currently living in a trailer park in New Jersey. Sad to relate, gravitas blunders are steeped in bias and inequity—but that doesn't make them any less real.

## HOW TO DEEPEN YOUR GRAVITAS

Gravitas is that je ne sais quoi quality that some people have that makes other people judge them born leaders.

But born leaders are made, oftentimes through their own systematic efforts. They live intentionally, guided by a set of values or a vision for their lives that compels them to seize every chance to put their convictions into practice. We gravitate to them because they telegraph that they know where they're going—a rare and intoxicating certainty that most of us lack. That is the real font of their gravitas.

So consider what larger vision you're here to fulfill, and make sure it informs each of your everyday actions. If you can articulate it, you're well on your way to achieving it. People with a clear goal who show they are determined to achieve it exude gravitas, which in turn bolsters their chances of securing the support they'll need to achieve their goals.

You can be one of them. Here are some quick wins and inspirational stories to get you started.

✓ *Surround yourself with people who are better than you.* "Best piece of advice I ever got," says James Charrington, chairman of Europe, Middle East, and Africa (EMEA) at BlackRock. "Recognize your own weaknesses, and hire people who will complement your strengths by addressing your weaknesses. Those I've seen struggle to move forward invariably are those who have trouble recognizing their shortcomings. When you talk about what you're not good at, it helps others see what you really are good at—and your gravitas grows for admitting it."

✓ *Be generous with credit.* As Deb Elam, head of diversity at GE, observes, nothing undermines followership faster than a boss who hogs all the credit for him or herself. Shining a light on those who helped you score a win underscores your integrity and sense of fairness, which in turn inspires others to give even more of themselves.

✓ *Stick to what you know.* Do not shoot from the hip; do not claim to know more than you do or possibly could know. Credit Suisse's Michelle Gadsden-Williams learned this back when she worked for a pharmaceutical firm and asserted to the executive committee that the playing field for black employees wasn't level. But she was careful to back up her assertion by offering concrete examples culled strictly from her own experience—and couched them as such. That way, she says, her insights were received as firsthand testimony and not a generalized indictment.

✓ *Show humility.* Nothing signals you're emotionally attuned more than your own willingness to admit mistakes and own up to failings and shortcomings.

BlackRock's Charrington doesn't hesitate to point out that he lacks a college degree, a very disarming revelation in this age of resume inflation and hyperbolic CVs. Facebook's Sheryl Sandberg likewise disarms detractors by volunteering embarrassing details of her seemingly flawless life, owning up to her seventy-pound weight gain during her first pregnancy ("Project Whale was named after me"), her failed first marriage ("No matter what I accomplished professionally, it paled in comparison to the scarlet letter D stitched on my chest"), and even her fear of being number two in her children's eyes ("Stay-at-home mothers can make me feel guilty and, at times, intimidate me").[29] Far from undermining her gravitas or tarnishing her reputation, her humility serves to bridge the gap between herself (the $1.6 billion woman) and her followers. It's hard to paint a mother who discovers head lice on her kids on the corporate jet as an out-of-touch billionaire.

✓ *Smile more.* This was advice Mellody Hobson received some twenty years ago from one of Motorola's most senior women. At the time, eager to demonstrate her toughness as a female on her way up, she was flabbergasted at the suggestion. Now she spreads the word. "Smiling a lot projects happiness and likability, and people want to work with those who they like and those who are happy," Hobson says. "There are energy givers, and energy takers. Who do you want to spend time with? Who are the people you run to the phone when they call and who are the ones you let go to voice mail? I want people to want to take my call."

✓ *Empower others' presence to build your own.* Others will see you as a leader when you concentrate on making

those around you act responsibly and win visibility for themselves, says Carolyn Buck Luce, a partner at accounting firm EY who recently retired. "Think about your impact, not in terms of deliverables, but in terms of realizing larger goals for the firm," she says. "See the bigger picture: You're a conductor of an orchestra. Executive presence is not what you do with your presence, it's also what you do with other people's presence."

✓ *Snatch victory from the jaws of defeat.* Steve Jobs did it when he reclaimed his role at Apple after an eleven-year hiatus during which his successor nearly ran the company into the ground. But perhaps the most notable exemplar of this is Al Gore, who was, for a few days in 2000, president-elect of the United States before the Supreme Court snatched away his victory. Ten years later Gore secured himself a Nobel Prize, and a place in history, that the presidency might not have conferred: as a prophet willing to speak an inconvenient truth, and as a visionary whom we entrust not only to show us the future but also to guide us safely through it. In so doing, he utterly transformed his image from a wooden lifelong public servant into a *Saturday Night Live* host with a devilish sense of humor as well as a disarming sense of humility. He is, as *New York* magazine put it, the ultimate Davos man, a leader whose credibility and gravitas are held in global esteem.[30]

✓ *Drive change rather than be changed.*

For the first thirteen years of her twenty-five-year run at Goldman Sachs, Gail Fierstein transformed the businesses she partnered with—first as a software developer, then as a project manager, then as a product line manager. It fell to Fierstein and

her team to solve some of the firm's thorniest challenges in terms of managing risk and introducing new product. "In tech, it's not just about innovating; you need to be thinking about worst-case scenarios and making sure they don't happen," she points out. "You've got to get into the detail, ask questions; you've got to keep challenging the group and your own assumptions."

But when she moved into human capital management as the Technology HR business partner, Fierstein's interrogative style didn't go over very well: "I'd ask about implementation, about how we were communicating, and how the team would support it because I was thinking twenty steps down the road. But either my colleagues in HR weren't used to getting questions or they didn't think my concerns about process were relevant, because to their way of thinking, I wasn't being supportive. I wasn't being a team player.

"That shocked me," she continues. "It was the complete opposite of tech, where the more questions you ask, the more you're considered part of the team, because it shows you're collectively working toward a solution."

So Fierstein stepped into the role of change agent. "You have to worry when I don't ask questions," she told her colleagues in HR. "And we all have to worry if you're not thinking twenty moves ahead." Subsequently, at every opportunity, Fierstein put a spotlight on her style difference. But at the same time, she says, she became more sensitive to the style differences of others. "Change works two ways," she observes. "In order to help others get to know me I provided them with context. I learned to say to junior people meeting me for the first time, 'I'm going to ask you a lot of questions. The more questions I ask, the more support I have for your proposal. So don't misinterpret my intent.'"

Her approach worked: Fierstein was promoted to managing

director and increased her span of responsibilities as HR business partner to eight divisions.

Today she's applying her toolkit to a whole new challenge, bringing women in the IT community together as a force for social good through her involvement with NPower, a nonprofit that harnesses the power of the tech community to bridge the STEM (science, technology, engineering, math) career gap for nonprofits. Once again, she says, she's bringing an execution/process mindset to the team. "Sometimes the very thing an organization wants you to change about yourself," Fierstein concludes, "is the very thing you most need to change about them." She adds, "When you acknowledge that, and start acting as a force for the greater good, others will follow your lead."

# 3

My first term as a student at Cambridge University was rough. I grew up in the coal mining valleys of South Wales and spoke English with a thick Welsh accent, whereas the vast majority of my classmates at Cambridge had attended elite public schools (Eton, Harrow, Cheltenham Ladies) and spoke impeccable "Queen's" English.

In class-conscious England, my South Wales accent indicated I was from the lower echelons of society. I dropped my aitches, talked about "our mam," and said "ta" instead of "thank you." Back in the 1970s these colloquialisms were not regarded as charming or cute. Indeed, my first week at Cambridge I overheard my tutor describe me to a colleague as "uncouth"—a memory that still makes me wince.

At bottom my accent signaled that I was uneducated or "ill-bred" (to use a particularly demeaning English term). And in a sense I was. I had very little knowledge of the world. My father occasionally brought home a local tabloid called the *Western Mail* but didn't see the point in buying a national newspaper, so I knew next to nothing about current affairs. Our household boasted a motley collection of nineteenth-century novels, courtesy of my mother, who loved the Brontë sisters, but outside of that I was not well-read. At eighteen I'd never been to the theater, shopped at a high-end store, or traveled abroad. We spent family vacations in

a trailer park in West Wales. As a result I had no small talk or cocktail patter. It wasn't a personality thing—I was friendly and outgoing. I was tongue-tied because I didn't have anything to talk about that suited my new milieu. I had no way of joining in conversations about, for instance, the Tory leadership struggle, the skiing season in Austria, or the latest in bell-bottom jeans.

My fellow students weren't openly rude or hostile—after all, they were "well-bred" young people—but they kept their distance. I wasn't on the invitation lists for sought-after freshman parties, and I found it impossible to penetrate the cozy circles that dominated the interesting clubs. I remember being the awkward, ignored outsider at the Cambridge Union (the university-wide debating society).

I soon realized that to survive and thrive I needed to strip myself of my accent and lose the most obvious of the class markers that set me apart from my peers. By January of that first year I was on the case and set about a transformation. I started with voice and speech—which were, after all, how I "betrayed" myself. I couldn't afford elocution lessons or a voice coach, so I bought a tape recorder and spent long hours listening to, and then attempting to copy, the plummy voices on BBC Radio. I sought out the newscasters on the BBC World Service since they spoke a particularly clear and neutral form of Queen's English. It took months, but I nailed it.

Concurrently I set about elevating my conversation so that it reflected the caliber of my thinking rather than my class background. I subscribed to the *Guardian* and the *Times Literary Supplement*, bought cheap tickets to the Arts Cinema, and plunged into the literature on African liberation movements. I was about to spend the summer in Ghana participating in a professor's research project, so why not develop some well-informed opinions about this intriguing continent? Africa was very "in." By June I

was trying out my newfound cultural and political fluency on my slowly expanding circle of sophisticated friends.

My makeover well under way, it was simply a matter of time before these improvements took and I could carry on conversations about a variety of topics without giving away my origins. This is not to say my struggle was over: For my family, my new accent was a different kind of betrayal, one that raised questions of authenticity (more on this in chapter 7). Yet the success I started to enjoy at Cambridge as a result of my transformation underscored for me two profound lessons. First, communication is not so much *what* you say but rather *how* you say it. And this you can condition and control. The tone and timbre of your voice; your choice and use of words; your inflection, articulation, and delivery; and even your body language determine what and how much your listeners take in—and what overall impression of you they will form and retain as a result. Other people's perceptions of you are very much yours to shape.

## ALWAYS ON

Most of us tend to think of communication skills in terms of formal presentation skills. But when are you not onstage? When are you not being judged? No matter what your job title or how junior or senior you are, you are always presenting. Whether it's a quick email to your boss, a casual comment you make to colleagues in the hallway, or a pitch you prepare for clients, you're conveying who you are and what authority is your due. In the real world and very much in the virtual one, every verbal encounter is a vital opportunity to create and nurture a positive impression. Your communication skills, both verbal and nonverbal, are what ultimately win you the attention and mindshare of colleagues, clients, and friends.

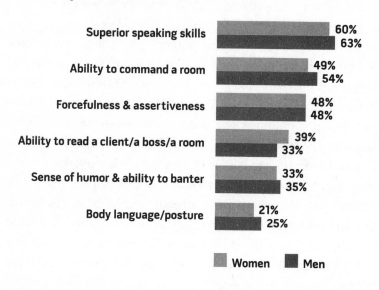

Figure 4. Top communication traits

In the arsenal of communication traits that confer executive presence—from how you stand to how you deliver your message—superior speaking skills above all mark you as a leader. Assertiveness and an ability to command a room emerge as critical tools as well. But less obvious things—such as your ability to read the room or banter with colleagues, even the way you hold yourself—contribute to your effectiveness as a communicator. These six behaviors boil down to one thing, really: How powerfully do you connect with your audience? How quickly can you engage your listeners, and how long can you keep their attention? Effective communication is all about engagement. And new research shows that, among the tools you bring to this task, content is the least

important aspect. A 2012 analysis of 120 financial spokespersons found that what makes a speaker persuasive are elements such as passion (27 percent), voice quality (23 percent), and presence (15 percent). Content matters a measly 15 percent.[31]

Effective communication turns out to be about the medium and not the message. Your topic may be of intrinsic interest, but unless you minimize distractions for your audience—no easy feat in this age of the omnipresent smartphones—you'll never manage to convey that interest. Look at the phenomenal popularity of TED talks, which spotlight some pretty arcane subjects. What makes a talk TED-worthy is not merely the topic but also the speaker's ability to engage the audience, in person and online, for eighteen minutes without the benefit of notes, PowerPoint, music, or lectern. It's no coincidence that what makes a great TED talk is a speaker who happens to employ masterfully all six of the core communication behaviors. To be heard above the din, to be seen despite the glitz, to be accorded authority and credibility, and to be remembered and heeded, you will need to master at least three of them.

## SUPERIOR SPEAKING SKILLS

Fundamentally, communication is about speech—a point made rather poignantly by Tom Hooper's Oscar-winning 2010 film, *The King's Speech*, which dramatizes the real-life transformation of Bertie (Albert), the stammering son of King George V, into King George VI after his older brother Edward abdicates the throne in 1936. Wife Elizabeth, keenly conscious of how her husband's speech disability undermines England's confidence in him as a leader, arranges for Bertie to work with a speech therapist whose tactics are decidedly unconventional. It's an agonizing and

humiliating process, but one that ends in triumph: Bertie over-
comes his stammer to deliver the radio address that crystallizes
the nation's resolve to take on Hitler.

Most of us, thankfully, don't have to contend with a crippling
stammer. But most of us do suffer from verbal shortcomings that
turn out to be just as damaging to our executive presence. Executives I interviewed cited inarticulateness, poor grammar, and an
off-putting tone or accent as examples of verbal tics that undermine EP. Other executives objected to "uptalk," the tendency of
younger women (and some men) to end declarative statements
on a high note, as if they were asking a question versus stating
a point. Still others complained of people who punctuated every
third word with "uh" or "you know." Everybody, it seems, recalled
an annoying voice, one that was too high-pitched or too mousy,
too breathy or too raspy. In particular, those we interviewed mentioned "shrill" women: women who, whenever they get emotional
or defensive, raise the timbre of their voice, turning off coworkers
and clients, and losing out on leadership opportunities.

These are verbal cues that can be adjusted. The painful part
is that you'll probably need to be told you've got a problem before
you can begin to address it.

## ACCENT

Top attorney Kent Gardiner, chair of law firm Crowell & Moring, recalls how, when he left his native Long Island, New York,
to work for the federal prosecutor in Texas, his mentor took him
aside to share some difficult advice. "You have to fundamentally
change how you speak," he told Gardiner. "You have to flatten
your accent. You have to work on it; you have to videotape yourself. You have to change, or you cannot survive in this state." Gardiner didn't seek outside help: "Nobody had any money, and the
government didn't have a program for rehabilitating New York

accents." But he did work on modulating his Long Island accent, and in doing so he developed the habit of listening to his own voice as he spoke. "Every time I speak to my partners, I think about it before I get up," he explains. "And as soon as I sit down, I re-listen to how the talk went. I just replay it mentally. It's very conscious. I work at it constantly, because nothing is more important in this profession than oral communication skills."

Sounding provincial can "destabilize your authority," says Gardiner. A British accent, on the other hand, does wonders for your gravitas, according to our focus groups, perhaps because speaking the King's English automatically sets you apart in global commerce, as a group of Standard Chartered managers told us in Singapore. "Maybe it's the weight of history or the depth of ancestry, but a British accent adds to the impression of heft," concurs Dr. Jane Shaw, former chairman of the board for Intel and former CEO of pharmaceutical giant Aerogen Inc. Before you rush out to acquire one, however, let me reference my own experience to point out that a British accent is complicated. There are good ones and bad ones, and even the good ones can get you into trouble, making you seem snobbish or even out of touch.

GRAMMAR

Sounding uneducated likewise undermines your gravitas and marks you as an outsider to the inner circle, as I discovered. Indeed, 55 percent of our respondents identified it as a top communication blunder. And yet it's the rare person who will risk correcting your word usage, as such correction calls attention to chasms of socioeconomic class, education, and ethnicity. Katherine Phillips, the Paul Calello Professor of Leadership and Ethics at Columbia Business School, describes how thankful she was to have found a sponsor who, early in her academic career, stepped in to correct her improper English. "You're saying the word wrong,

Kathy," her sponsor, who was her thesis advisor, told her. "It's 'ask.' Not 'aks.'" Reflects Phillips, who is African-American: "A lot of white people would be concerned they'd sound racist if they pointed these things out to an African-American colleague, but she realized the deleterious impact of how I spoke on other people—and on my career."

## TIMBRE AND PITCH

The research is overwhelming. Not only does the sound of your voice matter twice as much as what you're talking about, as the 2012 Quantified Impressions study of financial spokespersons found,[32] but a voice in the lower-frequency range will encourage others to see you as successful, sociable, and smart, according to a 2012 study published in the *Journal of Voice*.[33] Our research confirms that a high-pitched voice, particularly for women, is a career-stunting attribute. Indeed, to hear our interviewees and focus group participants tell it, nothing is more destructive of a woman's EP than shrillness. Crowell & Moring's chairman Kent Gardiner told me of his travails with a female litigator whose tone was so strident and shrill that the client demanded she be taken off his case. Lynn Utter of Knoll described the "fingernails on a chalkboard" effect of a senior female leader who was well-spoken and effective until emotion got the better of her, causing her voice to rise to a shriek—"and then everybody tuned her out." And here's why: "Shrill voices have that hint of hysteria that drives men into a panic," says Suzi Digby, a British choral conductor and music educator. "Women with a high-pitched tone will be perceived as not only unleaderlike but out of control."

Margaret Thatcher was fortunate to grasp and act upon this insight early in her political career. As a new appointee to Edward Heath's cabinet in 1970, she was pilloried for having, as one journalist put it, the "hectoring tones of the housewife."[34] When

the BBC dropped her from a political spot because her voice was too harsh, Thatcher recognized her career might depend on fixing that voice. So she turned to Hollywood voice coach Kate Fleming, who'd given Laurence Olivier the lower-register tones that established his gravitas in *Othello*. From 1972 until 1976, Fleming worked with her, transforming what biographer Charles Moore called "her annoying shrieking" into the voice that won her Heath's seat as prime minister in 1979 and helped establish her as Britain's Iron Lady, a woman renowned for "a smoothness that seldom cracked."[35]

Modulating a shrill voice is not a matter of learning to sound more like a man, but rather of achieving what scientists at Duke University have discovered to be an optimally pleasing sound frequency of around 125 Hz.[36] Human beings are apparently wired to tune into lower frequencies; and of course, we tend to pay attention longer to voices we don't find irritating. Consider whom you'd rather hear speak at your son or daughter's commencement: James Earl Jones (85 Hz)[37] or Roseanne Barr (377 Hz)?[38]

And if that doesn't incentivize you to bring down your pitch, this should: Optimally pleasing voices win the biggest leadership roles and earn the biggest salaries. Duke University's Fuqua School of Business and the University of California, San Diego's Rady School of Management analyzed recordings of 792 U.S. chief executives at public companies as they made investor presentations or earnings calls. They also gathered data on their salaries, length of tenure, and company size. After controlling for experience, education, and other influential factors, the scientists found that a drop of 22 Hz in voice frequency correlated with a $187,000 bump in compensation and a larger company size ($440 million larger, in fact). The implication? The lower your voice, the greater your leadership presence, which correlates to an increased likelihood of running a large company and making a substantial salary.[39]

You may think your voice isn't very mutable. But as Thatcher's experience demonstrates, with the right help you can modify it so that, at the very least, you don't turn colleagues off or drive people from the room. Speech training and coaching can make a difference, often because they provide what your colleagues or superiors just won't dare: feedback on how you sound. You may think you know how you sound, but you're not the best person to judge, as a recent *Wall Street Journal* article pointed out, because you hear your voice only after it's traveled through the bones of your head.[40] You may also imagine there's nothing wrong with your voice because no one's told you there is. But as we'll explore in chapter 6, unvarnished feedback is hard to give and hard to receive. Indeed, new consulting companies are springing up in response to client demand for feedback on just these sorts of matters; confronting a coworker or subordinate about speech issues is so fraught that few actually dare do it or manage to be constructive in their criticism.

So ask for feedback. A sponsor or mentor should be able to give you a good sense of what you need to work on. Then get to work—because a lot is at stake.

## COMMAND A ROOM

Say what you will about Arianna Huffington's politics, but she knows how to command attention—whether her audience is a room full of left-leaning movie moguls or a voting bloc of religious conservatives. With the *Huffington Post*, she commands a readership of some 5.7 million devotees per *day*.[41] Powerful people as well as the hoi polloi hang on her every word. What exactly is it about Arianna that makes her such a commanding presence?

Erik Hedegaard, who profiled Huffington for *Rolling Stone*

in 2006, suggests it's her "capacity for intimacy." Other profilers have stressed her seductive charm, a Bill Clinton–like capacity for making the listener feel as though he or she is the most interesting person in the room. And then there's her voice and accent—that mesmerizing overlay of erudition, honed during her student days at Cambridge, commingled with Greek sensuality.[42]

But it comes down to this: Arianna is never boring. And if you aspire to lead, you, too, must mesmerize your audience—or, to use the language of our survey research, "command a room," whether that room be a TV studio, a concert hall, or the team hang-out space. Nearly half of our respondents said it enhances a woman's executive presence, and more than half said it enhances a man's.

So: How do you grab and keep an audience?

## ESTABLISH CONNECTION

According to British choral conductor Suzi Digby, you've got all of five seconds to "touch the audience," or get them to invest in your message. It's all about making yourself human, she says: not oversharing, not indulging in self-revelation, but unveiling just enough of your inner core that your listeners feel connected to you and start pulling for you. Ironically, this can prove difficult for women, who find it easy to be forthcoming in private but are often self-consciously withheld in public settings, Digby points out. But getting an audience to like you, to root for you, while at the same time giving the impression that you don't *need* to be liked—this is the wire you want to walk.

I can speak to the power of this. At a large conference in Los Angeles sponsored by GE's Hispanic leaders, I delivered a keynote that presented CTI's cutting-edge findings about the challenges confronting Latinas in the U.S. labor market. While I was confident the research could withstand scrutiny, I was

conscious that I might not: Here I was, an elite-sounding English speaker appearing before them as an authority on Hispanic issues. So I didn't launch right into the research when I took the stage. Instead I shared my own story: how I struggled to overcome my accent and the issues I faced as someone born a girl child on the wrong side of the tracks. The effect this had was quite magical. In minutes I felt a palpable dissolution of tension as my audience put aside any reservations they may have had to join me in better understanding the research I wanted to bring to their attention.

### DELIVER YOUR WORDS AS A MUSICIAN DELIVERS NOTES

Phrasing, inflection, and pace are what distinguish you as a person worth listening to, says Suzi Digby. As in music, it's important to deliver your words conscious of your narrative arc, lifting and dropping your cadence to emphasize key passages or points, paying particular attention to how you end a phrase—what musicians call "phrasing off"—so that your listener senses closure and consequently hangs on to the last word and retains it before making room for the next. The uplift that younger speakers impose on the ends of their sentences, she observes, "undermines their whole message" by denying this closure.

The speed with which you deliver words impacts, in turn, the effectiveness of your phrasing. Digby, who in addition to leading the Queens' College choir coaches those selected to read passages from the Bible, says she's always amazed at how often eminent leaders rush their delivery. "Ninety-eight percent of the time even a good speaker will go way too fast trying to cram things in," she says. She coaches them to slow down, but also to surround the text with pauses and silences to heighten their power—again, a tactic composers employ to heighten drama and emphasize preludes and codas. "A musician's impact lies in the rests," she explains. "It's the

moment where you establish the tension and the seduction. Don't be afraid of silence."

I've seen this advice put to powerful effect by Sallie Krawcheck, who has learned to command the room by *not* speaking. "There is nothing so powerful as silence to make people sit up in their seats," Krawcheck told me. "It's loud. It's unexpected. It's dramatic. And it's confident." Then to demonstrate the effect, she paused a full second before adding, "*Very* confident." Deliberate silence is a trick she learned sitting at boardroom tables with titans like Sanford "Sandy" Weill, Vikram Pandit, Dick Parsons, and Robert Rubin, where men, she says, were accustomed to getting heard by being the loudest, most expletive-inflected voice in the room. To stand out as a woman, and to give heft to her thoughts, she started to punctuate her weightiest words with silence. "Those spaces give gravity to your most important pieces of advice, your most important insights, your most important messages," she explains. "It heightens drama because people are literally hanging on your words."

## USE NARRATIVE

Stories, not bullet points, are what grab and hold an audience. Ronald Reagan, an actor by training, earned the sobriquet "the Great Communicator" because he was a colorful storyteller and natural entertainer, not because he wielded facts like a policy wonk. Unfortunately, most newcomers to the stage attempt to establish their gravitas by aping the policy wonk rather than the actor. It's a common mistake among both men and women, particularly young professionals, to assume that an exhaustive and fact-laden presentation will bolster their gravitas, when in fact it does just the opposite: Going by the book underscores a lack of self-confidence and highlights an absence of individual spark. Remember, it's the TED talk, and not an MIT nuclear physics seminar, that you're trying to replicate.

### DON'T SNOW PEOPLE WITH DATA

Though she holds a Ph.D. in Asian studies, Rohini Anand, Sodexo's global chief diversity officer, has learned to be highly selective with how she delivers her messages, especially the positioning of facts and figures when presenting to different audiences. In some parts of the world, including her native India, she says, "you build up to your conclusion with data," whereas in the United States, "people just want your conclusion, the bottom line." So rather than build to the point, she gets to it quickly and limits herself to just a few data points that support what she's saying. Getting to the Q&A quicker, she finds, boosts interaction and ultimately provides her the platform to share her data.

Coming from academia myself, I experienced a learning curve similar to Anand's. My communication style after years of teaching at Barnard College and Columbia University was to present lengthy, nuanced arguments supported by a ton of compelling facts in fifty-minute chunks of time. Unfortunately, that style, which had won me a Teacher of the Year award at Barnard, went over like a lead balloon in corporate America. Business executives, I belatedly understood, have short attention spans: It's imperative you cut to the chase, be highly selective with your data, and whenever possible share an illustrative story.

### GET RID OF PROPS

Last year, less than a month after my friend Elaine was passed over for a C-suite promotion, I moderated a panel of executives that included the firm's chief financial officer. He knew that Elaine and I had worked together, so I asked him why she hadn't made the cut. After all, she'd been with the company twenty-five years and had an incredibly impressive track record.

He nodded, not in the least surprised by my inquiry. "She was one of the top three contenders for the job; indeed, in some ways, she was the most qualified," he affirmed.

Emboldened, I persisted. "So why didn't she get it?"

He sighed. "You're not going to believe the real sticking point, Sylvia, but you and I have known each other a long time and I'll come clean—the poor woman just makes too many lists."

I was bewildered—what was he talking about? Seeing the puzzled expression on my face, he tried to explain:

"Picture this," he said. "At our monthly executive committee briefing Elaine would always whip out a long list and meticulously consult it. Instead of looking you in the eye and talking compellingly about her team's wins and losses, she'd have her head in lists, notes, or some dreary PowerPoint. It's as though she didn't command the material—or trust herself to remember the thrust of her presentation. Now, you and I know she's as sharp as a razor and knows her stuff cold, but she doesn't present that way. She comes across as some kind of glorified executive assistant."

My eyes must have widened, because he added, "We can't put her in front of the board. We can't trust her with our important clients. Don't you see? It's about her ability to impress as well as perform."

As our focus groups affirm, constantly referring to lists, reading your notes, using eighty-seven PowerPoint slides, shuffling papers or flip charts, and putting on your glasses the better to see what you're reading are all actions that detract from your gravitas because they focus attention on your lack of confidence. If you cannot command your subject, you certainly won't be able to command the room. Know your material cold so that you needn't rely on notes, and needn't rely on your glasses to read notes. This will free you up to establish eye contact with the audience. And nothing is more important than eye contact, says Credit Suisse CEO Brady Dougan,

because it telegraphs to your audience that you're utterly in the moment. "There are such multiple tugs on people's attention that distraction is the norm," he observes. "Eye contact shows I have your complete attention, which I deeply appreciate because it's so very rare. In an important meeting, nothing boosts your leadership presence more than signaling that you're totally present."

### BE SUCCINCT

"Executive presence is not necessarily about being formal or abundant in your communication, but rather straightforward and brief," says Kerrie Peraino, head of international HR for American Express. "The more you keep speaking, or explaining yourself, the more you cloud or dilute your core message." Women seem especially prone to this blunder, she observes, perhaps because they're less sure of how they're perceived and seek to prove their expertise by overselling their case. According to Moody's Linda Huber, women also feel compelled to validate what they have to say by invoking all the people they consulted. "They go through five conditional clauses before they get to the point," she observes. "It's okay to say, 'I have a different point of view,' and then back it up with two or three reasons you can support with data. Don't start with, 'I've spent hours staying awake thinking about this and talked to thirty-seven people.' Get to the point, and then people will give you their attention."

## ASSERTIVENESS

When Barbara Adachi was promoted to regional head of Human Capital Consulting at Deloitte—the first woman to win such a position at the accounting/consultancy firm—she asked a partner we'll call Doug if she could sit on the firm's management com-

mittee with the other business leaders of audit and tax. He told her the seat was occupied by the regional director she'd reported to, who wasn't about to give it up. "We can't have two people from Human Capital at the table," he added. Adachi persisted. "But I'm a *partner* and now leading this region," she said. The other partner shook his head. "But people just don't see you as a leader, Barbara."

It was like a punch to the gut, Adachi recalls. A million responses came to mind, she says, including just storming out of the room. Instead, she managed to retort, "That's because I'm not on the management committee!" Doug laughed, and conceded she had a point. "That broke the ice with him," she relates. "But I could see his point, too: I wasn't viewed as someone who was well connected with other leaders in my region and office. I didn't have a powerful circle of sponsors, either. I may have been a partner, but nobody perceived me as one because I did not project executive presence."

So Adachi, a Japanese-American woman who was raised to listen, not talk, made a decision that would change her life. She went back to Doug and delivered an ultimatum. "If the regional director won't step down from the management committee, then I don't want to be the leader in Northern California, because I'd have all the responsibility and none of the authority. To do this job well, I need to be respected as a leader. And if I can't be on the committee, then I won't be viewed as a peer by the other leaders."

Ultimately Doug put her on the committee.

Being forceful and assertive is a core executive trait, for both men and women (as 48 percent of our survey respondents agree). But for women, it's a decidedly more difficult trait to embody, as assertiveness in a woman often makes her unlikable (the B-word is rolled out and she's seen as overly aggressive). We'll explore this tightrope walk in depth in chapter 6; here let's review some of the

strategies that apply to both men and women in terms of being effectively forceful.

Adachi feels in that moment of confrontation she proved herself a leader by arriving at a bold decision and showing she was ready to act on it. "I wasn't making an idle threat," she explains. "I was willing to walk away from the leadership role because having the responsibility without the authority would be comparable to being asked to hit a home run without a bat. And he saw and heard my resolve."

But she may also have prevailed because she framed her demand in the context of the good it would do the company, observes Rosalind Hudnell, vice president of human resources at Intel. "Push back," she counsels, "but try and avoid the I-word. Come from a position that's not about you, but about what's best for the company. Don't yell, and be careful about your tone. Because when you're working for a company, you're responsible to that company." The challenge is to keep that in mind while finding your authentic personal voice.

The executives I interviewed uniformly suggest you resist the urge to charge in and make known your demands. "You're not going to get anything done by asserting, 'This is what I want and I want it now,'" cautions a former Lehman Brothers executive who had worked with the company's CFO. "[The CFO] was never one to lack voice: She was brilliant on so many topics, and she enjoyed letting others know it," he recalls. "But in her new role, which she knew others begrudged her because she wasn't an investment banker, she overplayed her hand. Maybe she wanted to prove she could be as tough as the boys, but she showed no respect, and given that these guys had built the firm, that was more than a little unseemly. I told her, 'If you want to be heard, you've got to be a little more deferential to those sitting around the table with you.'"

Sensitivity can spell the difference between sounding like a leader and actually succeeding as one, as one female executive discovered when confronted with a labor crisis that threatened to go nuclear. Some four hundred of her employees didn't get their correct biweekly salary because of a payroll glitch. With her firm in the midst of union negotiations, she knew that this vendor mishap could trigger an employee action or work stoppage or devolve into a PR nightmare. So she got on the phone with the business leader, his team, and the local HR leader, and listened as they laid out the scope of the problem. Then she crafted a one-two punch. She laid out a nonnegotiable goal and assured the team she would support them in reaching it. "I am committed to seeing this through with you," she told the team on the phone. But after the call, in a one-on-one conversation with her colleague in charge of the vendor relationship, she made clear that his job was on the line, as his and her reputations were at stake. "I knew that demolishing this guy in front of everybody would not get me the cooperation I needed to resolve the crisis quickly," she observed. "So I allowed him to save face with his team, and then, behind the scenes, let him know that he was totally accountable." Her approach succeeded. The employee pay issue was resolved.

The best strategy for women may be what Linda Huber of Moody's describes as "leading from behind." In a room full of men, women often feel impelled to assert themselves by launching the first salvo. But far more effective, says Huber, an army officer who at age twenty-one had forty-five soldiers in her command, is holding off until others have fired off their best shot. "I learned a lot about military tactics from my father, who was a two-star general," she explains. "Even so, when it came time to do sand-table exercises of moving units around and practicing tactics, I was careful to wait, step back, and let others go first before offering up my solution." Having watched "a lot of cocky West Point

types blow up," she adds, she realizes that "sometimes it's best to sit back and listen, first."

Just make sure, when all eyes are upon you, that you do, in fact, offer a solution. A health-care leader described to me how, early in her tenure, she tried to get a team of scientists and engineers to agree on a way forward by eliciting everyone's opinion. Instead of reaching consensus, the room devolved into chaos. "Now I step up and say, 'Okay, we're not going to talk about this anymore,'" she explained. "'Here's the decision I've come to, and here's why we're going with it.' It could be the wrong decision—I've made those, every leader does. But at least you're making it."

And *that*, she adds, is what marks you as someone others will follow.

## ABILITY TO READ A ROOM

In early 2013 I was invited by Tulane University's Newcomb College Institute to be its annual Alberto-Culver Speaker, an endowed lecture series that invites high-profile women leaders to campus to talk about cutting-edge issues facing women in business. Given the publicity and branding around this event, I went to New Orleans expecting to address a sizable crowd. And in fact the venue was an auditorium at Newcomb College that easily held four hundred. But minutes before I took the stage I looked out and realized, to my dismay, that given the paltry trickle of students entering the lecture hall I'd be lucky to have fifty attendees.

In fact, there were thirty-eight—I counted them.

For any public speaker—politician or executive, professor or celebrity author—this is a sickening challenge. It's hard to exude executive presence and engage a crowd when, having prepared a speech for the National Mall in Washington, D.C., you arrive on

the Capitol steps to find that one earnest busload has shown up. Here I was, armed with a thirty-slide deck and a speech rehearsed for hundreds. What to do? I had minutes to decide.

My host, oblivious to the size of the turnout, hastened to the podium, donned her glasses, and read a lengthy introduction of me from a script she'd prepared. Some of those in the back of the auditorium got up and headed for the doors. Realizing that the rest of the audience might well slip away, I walked resolutely to the front of the stage and asked that everyone gather themselves into the first few rows. I asked for a chair, and sat myself down directly in front of them. Abandoning my PowerPoint, I addressed myself to them directly, communicating the essence of my data but relying mostly on narrative to pass the hour. I told many more stories than I'd intended, and at each natural break, I invited the students to ask questions—which they did, with eager energy. By the time we concluded the session, I felt a powerful connection. They felt it, too, because the evaluations they turned in were uniformly hyperbolic with praise. To this day I recall that event at Tulane as one of my most effective presentations, not despite my extemporizing, but because of it.

To command a room, you've first got to *read it*. Sensing the mood, absorbing the cultural cues, and adjusting your language, content, and presentation style accordingly are vital to your success as a communicator, and succeeding as a communicator is vital to your executive presence. Deploying your emotional intelligence and then acting on what it tells you absolutely boosts your EP—especially if you're a woman. Indeed, 39 percent of respondents told us this emotional-intelligence skill mattered for women, whereas 33 percent said it mattered for men.

Being oblivious to the needs of your audience will undermine perceptions of your authority. Here's why: First, it intimates you're a closed circuit, someone who can't or won't take in new

information (the woman who introduced me at Newcomb College being a prime example). Second, it implies you don't care about your audience, destroying any chance of connection, which is after all the foundation of any communication. Finally, and most damning, it implies you're simply not nimble enough to adapt to rapidly changing circumstances. Agility in a leader is increasingly prized in a global economy characterized by relentless change and persistent volatility.

What does it take to effectively read a room? You've got to tune yourself out in order to tune in to the needs and wants of others, and then course-correct on the spot to establish connection. Demonstrating that willingness impresses people: It shows you have absolute command of your subject matter, and it signals to your audience that you're so invested in the importance of your message that you'll scuttle your carefully prepared speech to make sure they grasp it. That's a recipe for engagement.

Sodexo's Rohini Anand recalls a particularly high-pressure meeting when she had one shot to convince the firm's top leaders to let outside experts advise the company on an extremely sensitive workforce issue. She entered the boardroom prepared to share the evidence she'd amassed, but in the end she elected to make her pitch with a short summary of the benefits, as she sensed the room wasn't interested in how she'd arrived at her insight. It was the right instinct: She made a convincing case, and within months Sodexo announced a new board of external advisors. "The tipping point in my career at this firm was when I figured out how to put myself in my audience's shoes and to paint a narrative balancing facts and stories depending on the audience," says this seasoned executive.

In this regard, professionals of color may hold an edge. In focus groups we conducted, countless participants confirmed that being a minority is itself a relentless exercise in reading others

in order to anticipate and overcome reflexive bias or unconscious resistance. Joel Tealer, an African-American senior vice president of human resources in the Strategic Business Units at Chubb Group of Insurance Companies, says that in order to maintain his EP, he adapts his speech to the culture of his listener and takes care to neutralize his political views, lest his mostly Republican colleagues take offense. "What you have to always do, as a multicultural manager, is make sure that you use the appropriate language for the appropriate situation," he says. "And during tough discussions, you have to be a bit more balanced because your audience can become less comfortable if you are viewed by them as a little bit left of balance, or overly animated."

That's not to say you compromise your views to pander to your audience, Tealer clarifies. "It's about making them comfortable," he says. "Reading your audience is all about winning their confidence so that when you speak, they really hear what you have to say."

## HUMOR AND BANTER

When Sallie Krawcheck offers up her analysis of what ails Wall Street, she pulls no punches. Whether it's the lack of oversight on money-market funds, the exorbitant executive compensation, or the absence of women in boardrooms, she serves up criticism heedless of blowback.

Yet precisely because she is dead serious, Krawcheck takes special care to leaven her critiques with humor. If women are stalled in their careers and need a leg up, for instance, it's because they're worn-out—exhausted by all the demands, professional and personal, placed upon them. "Do the math," Krawcheck exhorts her audiences. "Women spend so much more time on personal

grooming than guys do. Take me. I spend more, but let's assume fifteen minutes a day, an hour and fifteen minutes a week, five hours a month, sixty hours a year, on hair and makeup, and I have not shaved my legs yet! I've not yet dyed my hair, there is no mani-pedi, the brows have not been waxed, I have not gone to yoga, I have not run, I have done nothing but my friggin' hair and makeup."[43]

I've heard this shtick from Krawcheck on numerous occasions, and I can attest that it never fails to break up the room in gales of laughter. However brutal her message—in fact, especially when her message is brutal—Krawcheck's reliance on humor endears her to her listeners, who then become open to some inconvenient truths.

Not everyone can pull off a funny story at the lectern, but everyone can learn to banter at the water cooler. Many of our focus group participants affirmed the importance of mastering the art of small talk. "It's the conversation *before* the meeting that establishes whether or not you're worth listening to *in* the meeting," one senior executive pointed out—a skill she refers to as "mastering the banter." It shows, she explained, that you're part of the larger conversation, someone who's "one of the tribe."

To be sure, because the language and interests of the dominant tribe tend to dominate casual conversations, women and multicultural executives often find themselves at a disadvantage. In the words of one African-American focus group participant, "I don't watch the same television shows as my colleagues. That makes it hard to chime in about the most recent episode of *Survivor.*"

Well, watching *Survivor* isn't likely to boost your EP. Yet as I found at Cambridge, it's critical you strive to be conversant on a host of topics, if only because you'll have the confidence to insert yourself into the casual conversations of your superiors. "You don't have to say you're a Giants fan or Democrat or a Republican; you

just need to know enough to add to the conversation," says Deb Elam, a vice president at GE. "It's all about forging a bond with people—one that you may need to lean on down the road."

## BODY LANGUAGE AND POSTURE

On her second day of work for a leading insurance firm, one female focus group participant recalls how she was taken aside after a staff meeting and chided for doodling and slouching in her chair. "I don't want to ever see that again," her new boss told her. "You should be sitting up straight, pulled up to the table, making eye contact, and taking notes. You should be paying attention!" She tried to assure him she had been listening. "It doesn't matter," he said, waving a hand impatiently. "What matters is that your behavior told everyone that you weren't."

Never underestimate the communicative power of body language. While 21 percent of senior executives we surveyed recognize that how you hold and carry yourself affects your EP, anecdotally the evidence around body language suggests a much greater impact. "People gauge your EP the second you enter a room: how confidently you walk in, how firmly you shake hands, how quickly you make eye contact, how confidently you stand," observes Deloitte's Adachi. "In those initial seconds, you're going to be judged on what they see, not what they hear, and your body language and poise are what they see first."

Consider how the U.S. presidential candidates conducted themselves while facing off during three nationally televised debates in 2012. Indeed, executive coach and body-language expert Carol Kinsey Goman actually called the election on the basis of President Obama's body language alone, especially during the third debate. "He looked more comfortable and sure of himself,"

she observed, "using the definitive palm-down gestures and wide 'steepling' gestures that show certainty. And he has a great genuine smile (a big likeability cue) that he flashed a couple of times tonight." Governor Romney did well, too, Goman noted. "But he perspired, swallowed frequently, licked his lips, stammered, and (about 58 minutes into the debate) gave a slight shudder that showed in his shoulders and upper chest—all indicators that he was under a high level of stress."[44]

Since people will be "reading you" the moment they lay eyes on you, take care to enter a room or take the stage with aplomb. Is your head up, your gaze focused straight ahead? Shoulders back but relaxed? Do you stride or shuffe? And do you look happy at this opportunity to engage? Or do you look like you're nursing an ulcer?

When Catherine, a corporate senior executive, enters a room, people don't even need to know she spent more than twenty years in federal law enforcement to accord her awed respect.[45] Tall and elegantly dressed, this African-American woman radiates gravitas in her posture, stride, and stance. "I've been told I don't demand respect, that my presence expects it," she says. "Some of that came from growing up in the South and having to fight and wrestle with a lot of issues. When you are the first black person in a school classroom or at a company meeting, you learn to walk in with that Condoleezza Rice attitude of having to be better than the best. That conditions everything. Because I walk into every meeting with that attitude, holding my head high, I leave a positive impression behind. People want me at their table."

An erect bearing also conveys respect for others. That's why your mother told you to sit up straight at the dining room table: to show deference to those around you. In the film *The Social Network*, Mark Zuckerberg, slumped at the deposition table, telegraphs volumes to the attorneys assembled around him. "It's hard

to root for someone who makes you feel as though you don't warrant his attention," a young law firm associate told me.

A number of recent studies find, however, that the most important benefit good posture confers is chemical: When you stand tall, feet planted solidly and somewhat apart, chest out and shoulders back, you actually trigger a hormonal response that boosts testosterone and lowers cortisol, the steroid released from your adrenal glands in times of stress, from your bloodstream. Amy Cuddy, a social psychologist at Harvard Business School, discovered this through a series of controlled experiments she conducted on her colleagues (findings she shared as a TED speaker).[46] While the hormones last only about fifteen to twenty minutes, the rush of well-being and confidence may trigger "a physiological cascade that lasts all day," says Dana Carney, a social psychologist at the University of California, Berkeley's Haas School of Business.[47]

While standing at attention bolsters your own self-confidence, it absolutely signals to others that you are paying attention—which, as we've discussed, is perhaps the keystone of all effective communication. To radiate presence you have to radiate that you *are* present. And as Brady Dougan points out, that's where many a would-be executive stumbles. Virtually every executive I spoke to talked about enormously able men and women who sabotaged their chances at a top job by conveying in gestures large and small an inability to remain present when it mattered most. Kent Gardiner, chided early in his career for checking his watch too often during meetings, says he's become a stickler about ensuring his colleagues don't commit similar blunders of inattention, including pen-clicking, foot-tapping, paper-rustling, and device-checking. Jane Shaw told me one of the rudest things she recently witnessed was a board member turning his back on the meeting in order to deal with some emails. Tuning out to consult your smartphone elicited some of the most heated discourse in our focus groups and

interviews, in fact. Sara, who works in derivatives and structured finance at Moody's, told us, "I really get annoyed when I see a handful of managers who think their time is more important than everyone else's, who don't hear what I am saying after I've spent weeks preparing. This behavior really undermines their executive presence in my mind. How can you trust a leader to keep his eye on the big picture if he can't keep his eye off his iPhone?"

## BLUNDERS

During her twenty-four years in Congress, Colorado representative Patricia Schroeder was lauded for her stalwart advocacy of work-family issues (she sponsored the Family and Medical Leave Act of 1993) and her tough stance on congressional reform. However, for many her name will forever be linked with bursting into tears on national television when she announced in 1987 she would not seek the Democratic nomination for president. "Women across the country reacted with embarrassment, sympathy and disgust," wrote the *Chicago Tribune* a week later.[48] *Saturday Night Live* lampooned her in a skit on the presidential primary debates.[49] More than two decades later, Schroeder told *USA Today*, she was still catching flak about it.[50] The verdict: Wiping away those tears erased the perception that Schroeder might have been fit to be the country's chief executive.

Crying is just one of a menu of communication blunders that, in a mere instant, can suck the executive presence right out of you. Others, as identified by our focus groups, include breathlessness or any other sign of nerves, constantly checking your iPhone for the latest messages, being obviously bored, being long-winded instead of getting right to the point, and relying too heavily on notes and other props. These flaws are fatal for one simple reason:

## Communication Blunders
**From focus groups and interviews**

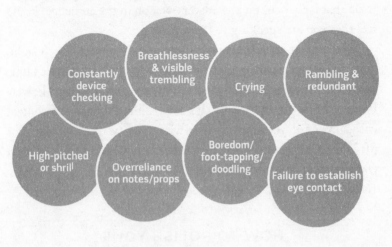

Figure 5. Communication blunders

Whether you're speaking to a small group or a large audience you need to fully engage your audience's attention, so that they both hear and remember your message.

Without helpful—although it might seem brutally honest—feedback from a colleague or boss, how can you tell whether you've buried your point in an avalanche of self-inflicted communications mistakes? There's an easy indicator: Listen for the "cough count." How many times does your audience feel compelled to cough or clear their throats? Similarly, check the "fidget factor." Are you spotting people shifting in their seats, crossing and uncrossing their legs, examining their nails or cuffs, or adjusting their arm positions on the tables or chairs? All of these things are a dead giveaway that your presentation is making them wish they were elsewhere.

Establishing eye contact is particularly important. When you start speaking, you want everyone focused on *you*—and the way to do that is to focus on *them*. Every person in the audience should feel that you are speaking to them.

Eye contact is, of course, dependent upon a clear line of sight. That means you need to lose the props—or at least a sizable number of them. Eyeglasses, podiums, notes, flip charts, and Power-Points can all get in the way. It's impossible to make eye contact with anyone if you're struggling with twenty pages of notes or fifty densely packed PowerPoint slides. The less there is between you and your audience, the better.

## HOW TO POLISH YOUR COMMUNICATION SKILLS

✓ *Ditch the verbal crutches.* Fillers such as "um," "like," and "you know" get in the way of and undermine your message. Tape yourself. Allow yourself to pause when you're giving thought to something mid-sentence. Moments of silence give greater import to the words that precede and follow them.

✓ *Broaden your small talk.* Kalinda, a real-estate analyst at a financial-services company, affirms the usefulness of being able to contribute to casual conversations: "One of best things ever to happen to me was managing the NFL budget," she says, referring to a former job. "I didn't know a thing about American football when I got there, but I recognized I needed to, if I was ever going to be considered one of the guys. So I read *Sports Business Daily* every day. The teams, the games, the analysts—I could talk about all of it with anyone.

Even now, if I hear football being discussed, I insert myself in that conversation, because I have something to add. For the same reason, I picked up golf a couple of years ago. I'm not good at it, but I can talk about it, and that opens a door with my managers."

✓ *Get control of your voice.* Lord Bell, the advertising guru and PR maestro who masterminded the British Conservative Party's 1978 campaign, helped tone down the Iron Lady's speaking voice with a simple concoction: water tinctured with honey and lemon. "Because she did so much talking, her vocal cords got stressed and it made her sound shrill," he says. "We found that if she drank some hot water with lemon and honey it lowered her pitch and took the strain out of her voice."[51] Sallie Krawcheck makes sure she breathes, consciously and deeply, before taking the stage, to eradicate any shakiness in her voice. Kerrie Peraino sips water to relax her throat muscles, as tight muscles can produce a squeaky, raspy, or breathy tone.

✓ *Overprepare.* Barbara Adachi finds that by dint of careful preparation, she can overcome her inclination not to speak unless spoken to. "I used to go to meetings and just not say a word," she recalls. "People wondered why I was even there. Unless asked to comment, I wouldn't volunteer. Speaking up was so hard for me. And I still need to push myself in new situations. But if I go in well-prepared and knowing I know more than I need to, I find it easier to speak up and not go back into my cocoon."

✓ *Less can be more.* Jane Shaw, former chairman of Intel's board, affirms that you can't afford to be a wallflower at meetings. But she cautions against speaking up just

for the sake of it. "Inject a comment when you have something fresh to add. If you're asked for an update, stick to new items. Invite others to add their opinion rather than babble on. If someone has not weighed in, you might throw it to them when you finish," she advises.

✓ *Invoke your vertical.* Anne Erni, who today heads up human resources at Bloomberg, describes an incident early in her career on Wall Street where her body language helped her pull off an unpopular decision with a hostile crowd. "The other executives were ganging up on me, literally yelling and cursing. Meanwhile, forty people were waiting for us to come forth with a decision. I had to focus on getting to that goal. I sat there and, with every ounce of energy, just kept pushing my feet into the floor, sitting tall, and making my spine and head straight. Then I leaned forward and spoke. It not only got me through that awful moment, but I won their confidence, and we moved forward."

✓ *Lose the props.* It bears repeating: You will exude executive presence if you establish and maintain a direct connection with your audience, whether you're addressing two or two hundred. Learn to present without props.

✓ *Do not allow challenges to your authority to go unanswered.* Hecklers are looking to rob you of your command of the room by getting under your skin. Don't let them. Parrying with humor is your best defense, as it demonstrates that your confidence can't be shaken and makes the heckler look petty for trying. You can also declaw a barb by acknowledging a germ of truth in it—and then annihilating that germ with counter-

evidence. Sometimes, however, it's important to reassert your authority by going full frontal. Dwight Robinson, chief of diversity at Freddie Mac, describes how his first sponsor chose him as his deputy to run the state housing authority committee. Robinson knew he was utterly qualified to win the position, but as both he and his sponsor were African-American, he knew the decision would come under fire. Indeed it did. But Robinson's sponsor did not flinch. To the builders, the developers, and the mayor who questioned his choice, he countered, "You've got twenty-seven other departments with two people of the same race in charge. They've solved their problems, so how does it signal something negative when two white people are running twenty-seven agencies and two black people are running one?" Robinson says it was a "life lesson" for him in exercising courage and asserting authority.

# 4

When we first met—at a wedding anniversary celebration for mutual friends—I was impressed and intrigued by D'Army Bailey. He radiated vigor and charisma. A few weeks later we got together for coffee and I learned much more about him. A Memphis-based lawyer and former judge, Bailey started out as an activist in the civil rights movement. He's had a remarkable career litigating and adjudicating landmark cases, writing two books, and ultimately founding the National Civil Rights Museum in Memphis.

But as we chatted and sipped on a second round of lattes, I couldn't help but marvel at his appearance. Fit, toned, and impeccably dressed, he looked impossibly young. I was perplexed. "How is it that you, a man who marched with Martin Luther King, looks not a day over forty-nine?" I asked him.

"I've had three plastic surgeries," he confessed nonchalantly. "I've had a forehead lift, a facelift, and had the bags removed from under my eyes."

My mouth fell open and I spilled some coffee.

Seeing my astonishment, he burst out laughing. "Why shouldn't I look my best?" he exclaimed, not in the least defensive. "I'm not ready to throw in the towel. I don't want to retire."

He then went on to explain that he'd long understood the connection between looking good and looking capable. "Facelifts and good dental work convey a more youthful appearance, but

they also signal confidence and credibility. To my clients I'm more trustworthy. To a jury I'm more believable. Now, don't get me wrong, my appearance isn't what wins me a case, but when I look in control I feel in control—and that's how others perceive me."

Keisha Smith, managing director and co-head of talent management at Morgan Stanley when I interviewed her, now at News Corporation, told me that it was quite by accident that she came by her signature look. After a dye job went wrong, she had a barber shave off her hair—and liked the result. In the years since, as she has moved up the corporate ladder into roles of ever greater visibility and responsibility, she has perfected her stand-out look.

Tall, with wide-set eyes and a dazzling smile, she's an executive you'd notice anyway; but as a bald Afro-Caribbean woman who holds a senior position at a Fortune 500 firm, she's a leader you'll never forget. It's not the shaved head so much as the statement it makes: that she's utterly at ease in her skin.

Smith is conscious that her appearance can "widen the gap" between herself and those she meets for the first time. In her words, "I'm aware that my aesthetic is unusual, and can be intimidating, which is why I take pains to close that gap by seeking out personal connections and establishing common ground with my colleagues." However, she explains, it's a style she enjoys, one that she intends to keep even if it does mean feeling self-conscious at every meeting with new clients. "I do what I need to do to make it work in my work environment, because having a style that I'm comfortable in breeds the inner confidence which helps me be successful." She adds, "I really wouldn't have it any other way."

D'Army Bailey and Keisha Smith underscore the complexities of the appearance challenge today. A seventy-year-old male jurist can talk openly about how plastic surgery has enhanced his ability to stay in the game, and a forty-year-old female exec-

utive can choose to be bald and have it contribute to her gravitas. But do these voices signal new freedoms or new constraints? We've learned to value authenticity—and this is good—but at the same time standards have risen and we're judged on many more fronts—wrinkles and waistlines as well as a well-cut skirt or suit.

As we wrestle with the thorny—and annoying—issue of looks, three things are uppermost in our minds: What marks us for success? What exactly are bosses and colleagues looking for these days? And how much does this superficial stuff matter anyhow?

At first glance, CTI data seems to show that appearance isn't that important. Sixty-seven percent of the senior executives we surveyed told us that gravitas was the core characteristic of executive presence; 28 percent said that communication skills comprised the core; and a mere 5 percent said appearance was at the heart of the matter. However, from our qualitative data we found that appearance was typically the *filter* through which gravitas and communication skills were evaluated. That explains why high-performing junior employees oftentimes get knocked out of contention for key roles and promotions: they simply don't look the part. In other words, get this appearance thing wrong and you're struck off the list. No one even bothers to assess your communication skills or your thought leadership capabilities if your appearance telegraphs you're clueless.

Over the long haul, the way you look may not be nearly as important as what you say or how you act, but it's incredibly important in the short run. Cracking the appearance code opens doors and puts you in play.

So what are senior leaders looking for? What are their top picks?

According to Senior Leaders

# Top Aspects of Appearance

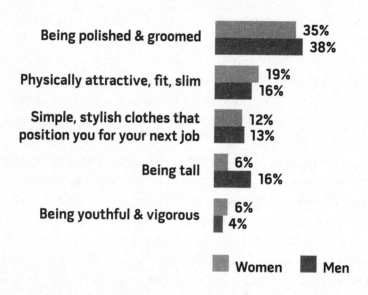

Figure 6. Top aspects of appearance

## BEING POLISHED AND GROOMED

I find this top pick extremely comforting because it confers on individuals a great deal of agency and control. More than a third of the senior executives in our survey (men and women) considered "polish and grooming" vital to men's and women's EP, whereas less than a fifth said that physical attractiveness matters. It turns out that the intrinsic stuff (body type, height) is not what matters most; rather, it's what you do with what you've got. As one leader put it in an interview, "You've got to look as though you tried, that you pulled yourself together." When I present this data most professionals are

relieved to learn that cracking the appearance code is something that can be learned and you're not stuck with what you were born with.

Research conducted by Nancy Etcoff at Harvard Medical School bears this out. She showed 268 subjects images of women's faces, either flashing the images for 250 milliseconds or allowing subjects ample time to study the images. As can be seen in the figure below, the images featured three women, each of them made up in four different ways.[52] The *only* difference between the four versions of each woman's face was the amount of cosmetics applied—the range was from no makeup to dramatic makeup.

Subjects were asked to assess each woman's face in terms of how attractive, competent, trustworthy, and likable they judged the woman to be.

## First Impressions

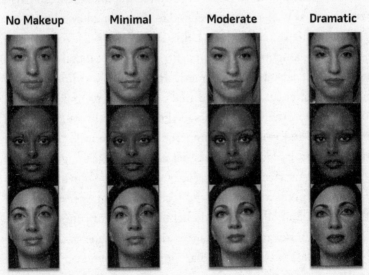

**Figure 7. First impressions**

What did Etcoff and her team find out? Not surprisingly, judgments about a woman's attractiveness were heavily conditioned by how much makeup she was wearing—the more, the better—and number 4 was the top choice. Much more startling, judgments about her competence, likability, and trustworthiness were also deeply affected by cosmetic choices. As though competence is really a function of how much lipstick you wear! Again, the rule of thumb seemed to be the more makeup the better. With one exception, the top choice for trustworthiness was number 3, not 4. This implies that although dramatic makeup gets high marks it's hard to fully trust a woman who looks glamorous.

One startling thing about this study is how quickly these judgments were made (250 milliseconds). And these flash judgments tended to stick. Even after viewers were given the chance of unlimited inspection and reviewed their decision, they continued to accord highest marks (in terms of competence, likability, and trustworthiness, as well as attractiveness) to the most adorned faces.[53]

Trying hard really does help. A judicious use of cosmetics, neatly manicured nails, well-fitting jeans (Silicon Valley), a perfectly cut jacket (Wall Street), and carefully coiffed hair all make a difference. When you make an effort to look polished, you signal to others that you see them as worth your time and investment, and you're even prepared to tolerate mild discomfort (think of those closely fitting shirt collars that rub against your neck or those stylish four-inch heels that cramp your toes). Who wouldn't respond to such efforts! It's a statement of respect, after all—respect for colleagues and clients, respect for yourself.

No one better understands this than my friend and coauthor Cornel West, the beloved scholar, philosopher, and activist who's much admired for his courage in speaking truth to power. To hear West deliver one of his passionate, powerful speeches is to experience something that rocks you to your core. And appearance is an

integral part of it.[54] Sure, there's his body language. He assumes a forward-pitched crouch, which frees up his arms to wave and gesticulate. There's his delivery, a song that crescendos into a battery of inconvenient truths before resuming its lulling cadence. And then there's West's "uniform," the black three-piece suit, black tie, immaculate white shirt (French cuffs flaring, cuff links glinting), black scarf, and silver-toned watch fob. I have never seen him attired in anything else. He wears this uniform whether he's sitting next to Newt Gingrich on a television stage, serving breakfast to the urban poor, or sitting in my backyard on a sultry August afternoon. While it doesn't always get him a taxi at night in New York City, West's look does command the attention of heads of state and business titans as well the loyalty and affection of millions of regular folk.

But there's more to his clothing than distinctiveness. West perceives his attire as his suit of armor, the thing that enables him to face the "bullets and arrows" endemic to his work. "It makes me feel good, to put on my uniform," he says, "because you've got to be ever ready for engagement and combat." If he's rather particular about the details of his uniform—the break of his cuff, the crease in his pants—it's because he cannot permit a breach in his self-confidence. "If I walk around without my crease, it's like walking around with my shoes not shined," he says. "I don't feel right."

West wears this uniform because it telegraphs, to himself and others, the seriousness of his mission and the respect he bears for those who launched him on his journey. His suits are akin to Martin Luther King's "cemetery clothes," which, West explains, MLK wore to remind himself that he was going to live and die for something bigger than he was. "I may be smiling, laughing, fighting, writing, and speaking—with hope, and kindness, and humor," says West, who these days is a professor of religious

philosophy and Christian practice at Union Theological Seminary in New York, "but I'm 'coffin-ready' because the tradition that produced me sets the highest standards that I could possibly aspire to."

Now, I'm not urging you to wear a three-piece suit or any other uniform. Nor do I wish to imply that polish can only be achieved by wearing black or nailing that crease in your pants. I am suggesting, however, that you take pains to signal, in your appearance, a seriousness of purpose by attending to the details. Casual clothes may be the right choice for your organizational culture, but in their fit and brand and style, they should telegraph that you take your work and those whom you engage in it very seriously. Poor grooming—dandruff on your collar, scuffed shoes, broken nails, runs in your tights, soup on your tie—compromises the ability of other people to see you as someone who's going places because it says that either you don't notice sloppiness or you don't care enough to attend to it. In interview after interview, senior leaders told me that failure to come through on the grooming front signals either poor judgment or lack of discipline. Neither is good.

"If you were making a pitch for a new piece of business, you wouldn't go into that client meeting with hand-scribbled notes," says Mark Stephanz, vice chairman of Bank of America Merrill Lynch. "No: You'd go to no end of trouble to be sure that you had a PowerPoint (or printed deck) at the ready which was polished, powerful, and error-free. And the same rules must apply to your presentation of self."

Good grooming is not just about making a polished first impression: It's about signaling to your competitors, and yourself, that you're in total control. Former judge D'Army Bailey told me he had his aha! moment about grooming back in high school, when he saw Jackie Gleason and Paul Newman star in *The Hustler*. What impressed him was how Minnesota Fats, the pool shark

played by Gleason, maintained his cool throughout a night of fearsome competition by going into the men's room during breaks to wash his face, comb his hair, and straighten his tie. "He wants his opponent to think he's fresh, and unfazed by the intensity of the challenge," Bailey observes. "I learned from this that in every encounter with an opponent, it's a psychological game you're playing, and no matter how tense you are, you should try not to show it. Don't let them see you sweat; don't allow yourself to look worn or unkempt." So Bailey gets regular facials and manicures, in addition to frequent haircuts. "If I am meeting with someone consequential and look down and see I'm two weeks out from a manicure, I'm going to start worrying about what is showing on my nails, and that's going to distract me," he says. "Tidy nails, a fresh haircut, and a fresh shirt always give me a confidence boost."

Achieving polish comes down to this golden rule: *Minimize distractions from your skill sets and performance.* Have professionals tend to your nails and hair regularly. Invest in well-cut attire that complements your body type. Accessorize, but don't billboard your bling. And unless you're in an industry that prizes physical beauty, don't flaunt your body. For men as well as women, sexuality scrambles the mind. Don't wear shirts that emphasize your build or blouses that emphasize your bust; avoid tight or skimpy trousers or skirts. Clothing that advertises your body steals attention from, say, your laser-sharp analytic skills or your visionary design expertise or your compelling oratory. All of which underscores one basic principle: Your appearance should focus your audience on your professional competencies, not distract from them.

Minimizing sexual distraction is especially important if you're female. A senior Wall Street executive who's mentored a number of high-flying women told me that oftentimes he's needed to spell out how and why dressing in a sexually suggestive way undermines a woman's EP. In his words: "When a female executive

walks into a room with three buttons open, a black lacy bra showing under her blouse, and a skirt hiked high, these things are going to distract the men sitting around a conference table ... and they will take you much less seriously, however big a producer you are." As he explained it to me, "It's not that I want my protégées to look less feminine, just less provocative." He then went on to speculate, "It's as though at a deep level, some women believe that the power they ultimately wield is their sexuality. But overt sexuality has no place in the executive suite."

Women, it seems, walk a fine line between turning heads and dropping jaws. So another rule of thumb: You should look "appropriate for your environment, and authentic to you," as Kerrie Peraino, head of international HR for American Express, puts it. A tongue stud may be authentic to you, she explains, but it's probably not appropriate to your environment unless you work in a tattoo parlor. Similarly, Dolce & Gabbana suits may be appropriate to your environment, but if glamorous designer wear doesn't speak to who you are, don't don the label. "Wearing clothes that feel inauthentic detracts from your internal confidence," says Peraino. "A look that isn't you—that has everyone scratching their heads—can actually sap your executive presence."

That's why the same dress on two different women can telegraph two completely different messages: It's not the clothing per se but *who you are* that determines whether it's appropriate. Peraino tells of a very senior leader at American Express, a woman who wowed everybody with her above-the-knee red dress when she took the podium at a recent women's leadership event. "It totally worked," says Peraino, "because she'd earned it. She was entitled to the red dress. She was hot—not because she was trying to be sexy, but because she really is powerful." Peraino thought for a moment and then added with a smile, "And that red dress had a conservative neckline. A little leg is one thing; cleavage is something else!"

PHYSICALLY ATTRACTIVE, FIT, SLIM

There's a plethora of research proving the point that intrinsically attractive people get a speed pass over life's bumpier transitions: They get hired more often, earn more, and even fare better in court than unattractive people.[55] But thankfully your executive presence doesn't depend on looking like a movie star. As I stressed earlier, grooming and polish count way more than conventional good looks (classic features, a well-proportioned body, abundant hair). But even with regard to physical attractiveness, what you do with your God-given gifts counts more than your intrinsic beauty in establishing your credibility as an up-and-comer.

The most important thing you can do, our qualitative data shows, is to signal fitness and wellness. It's not how much you weigh, but how resilient you seem that enhances or detracts from your executive presence—because leadership is demanding. We tend not to entrust our toughest jobs to people who look like they might keel over from a heart attack. "Being physically fit gives people the confidence that you will take care of what you are asked to do, because you are taking care of yourself," notes GE executive Deb Elam.

This helps explain why Chris Christie, New Jersey's popular and portly governor, took the drastic step of undergoing lap band surgery in early 2013. Irrespective of his political ambition, he told reporters, he had to address his weight; it was a health issue, not an image issue. And yet health *is* the image issue when we're talking about the nation's highest office. Estimated at over three hundred pounds, Christie recognized that his weight might distract voters from his more important attributes and accomplishments.[56] To make a successful presidential run, he cannot be obese. Obama, who is two inches taller than Christie, weighs 180 pounds.[57] He's far more typical of chief executives these days.[58]

Telegraphing fitness is all the more important if you're heavyset

and female, because women, our research affirms, suffer more from fat stereotypes than men. Both men and women with larger waistlines and higher body-mass-index readings tend to be perceived as less effective in terms of both performance and interpersonal relationships,[59] and "lacking in confidence, self-discipline, and emotional stability."[60] But weight is held against women more than it's held against men: 21 percent of the senior executives we surveyed believe that being overweight detracts from a woman's executive presence, while only 17 percent believe it detracts from a man's EP. "There's definitely more latitude for overweight men," says one manager I interviewed who's struggled with her own weight. "Generously proportioned women are just seen as unprofessional. It's a third-rail kind of thing, so it doesn't ever get mentioned in performance evaluations. But do people with excess weight advance at the same rate as those without? I suspect the answer is no. There is bias." In our focus groups, both male and female executives echoed this observation. "Women who are overweight are seen as out of control and lazy," one banker told us.

Unless you're obese, the takeaway here is not to embark on a body makeover campaign. Rather, it's to pay more attention to how well (as in healthy) you look, and how well you look after yourself. Whether you're a size 16 or a 6, get enough exercise to ensure your muscles are toned and your lung power will see you up stairs without wheezing. Put extra effort into your grooming and polish; make sure your clothing fits your actual size, not the size you're hoping to be. Looking well put together demonstrates respect for yourself and your organization. In the end, that's what impresses.

SIMPLE, STYLISH CLOTHES THAT POSITION YOU FOR YOUR NEXT JOB

The platinum pixie, the gauntlet of silver bangles, the Prada dress or Balenciaga leather leggings—this is Joanna Coles, editor in

chief of *Cosmopolitan*. She has an amazing signature look and personal brand, one that's totally working for her in her highly visible role at the helm of the world's most notorious magazine. She's gotten roles playing herself on *The Job* and mentoring fashion designers on *Running in Heels* and *Project Runway All Stars*; she's gotten in front of the camera on MSNBC's *Morning Joe* to share her insights on how to interview for a job, and been snapped simply for chatting up Miley Cyrus (and outdressing her) at the Rachel Zoe runway show.

But this wasn't always Coles. It's been a longish journey, figuring out her look. As a young journalist, and the author of an interview column, her role demanded she be all but invisible. "It really wasn't about me, but rather about the person I was interviewing," she explains. "I would wear black or navy pants and a black or navy jacket; I would try and look as reassuring as possible and ease into the background."

When she left her reporter job for an editing role, Coles experimented with her hair, dyeing it red and wearing it long—a trademark look, to be sure, but not one that telegraphed the seriousness of purpose she felt or the ambition that drove her. Only when she became editor of *Marie Claire* and had to make many public appearances did Coles effectively leverage her fashion smarts to magnify her executive presence. "In my twenties and thirties I worried that if I looked as if I spent time on my appearance I would appear vain and unserious," she says. "But fashion has changed, there are more options for women, and I now realize had I spent more time on it, it might have given me more authority."

We're all on this journey. We're either searching for our signature look, refining it, or reinventing it, because visibility is hard to maintain in our ever more competitive world economy. To be sure, the older you get and the higher you go, the more latitude

you'll have—Steve Jobs, as we all remember him, wore nothing but black turtlenecks and blue jeans. But those whom we recognize today for their signature look have nonetheless spent years working on it and earning it.

The journey begins by dressing for the job you *want*, not the job you have.

Kalinda, the real-estate analyst, remembers her "uniform" when she was working as a financial analyst for a cable sports channel. She had adopted the casual attire typical of staffers who weren't in front of the cameras: jeans, T-shirts, and sweaters. On the advice of a mentor, she traded in her aggressively casual attire for tailored slacks and blazers. "I looked great, and I felt more confident," she admits. Her superiors agreed. A few months after her makeover, Kalinda was put in charge of a major launch and given oversight of a new hire. "I'd been asking for this sort of thing, and my performance had always been strong," she says. "But only when I started dressing for the part I wanted, instead of the part I had, did others perceive me as ready for that step up."

Complement a sophisticated look with a signature style piece or accent. For men this might be a pair of colorful socks, a playful tie, vintage cuff links, distinctive shoes, or a bold watch. Women have arguably more options. Margaret Thatcher so famously wielded her Launer handbag that *handbagging* became the term used for Thatcher-style strong-arming of political opponents. Madeleine Albright adorns every suit with a quirky brooch. Cornel West leavens his ministerial look with a carefully maintained Afro. The more rigorous the dress code, or the more wholeheartedly you embrace it, the more it behooves you to personalize it in some standout way. The most successful signature looks convey that you know what's expected of you and willingly embrace it—yet have the self-possession to channel your individuality through it.

Remember that your signature look encompasses not just you

but also the physical space you occupy. Your office, like your body, is a vehicle for your brand. Just look at top executives' offices and you'll see how they affirm their image and trumpet their brand in their choice of furnishings and objects. For example, black-and-white fashion photographs cover every square inch of wall (and windowsill) in *Vogue* editor Anna Wintour's office, but the understated color scheme (white, glints of gold and silver, a glass desktop) ensures that the overall effect is, like Wintour herself, sleek, sophisticated, and stunning. In contrast, Nike CEO Mark Parker conducts business in a space that's so crammed with bad-boy posters, toys, prototypes, pop art, and kitschy memorabilia it's a wonder he can work in it. I certainly couldn't. But that's not the point: Parker portrays himself as an extension of the Nike brand, rather than a contradiction. In very real ways, CEOs *are* the public face of their companies, and they are well-advised to align their brands with that of the business they represent.

## BEING TALL

Michael Dukakis, the Democratic nominee for president in 1988, will go down in history for two things: the infamous tank photo, in which the would-be commander in chief looks like he's been vanquished by a headset, and his height, which was something less than the five feet, eight inches he claimed on his driver's license.[61]

George H. W. Bush, who was six feet one, beat him handily, despite his own image issues ("Our Wimp Can Beat Your Shrimp," declared one Republican bumper sticker), because shortness in a male leader was and is so easily conflated with major shortcomings. "Shortness creates a presumption of weakness," writes Ben Shapiro, author of *Project President: Bad Hair and Botox on the Road to the White House*, noting that Dukakis was seen as seriously weak on defense and weak on crime.[62]

If women's leadership potential is unreasonably correlated to

weight, men's is unfairly correlated to height. Sixteen percent of our respondents said height contributed to men's EP; only 6 percent said it contributed to women's. This bias most visibly plays out in presidential contests: Since Dukakis ran for the office, every man to sit behind the Oval Office desk has been taller than six feet. Over the history of presidential contests, taller candidates have beat out shorter ones 17 to 8.[63]

What to do if you're among the height-challenged? In this regard women have one killer app to help them compensate: high heels. And they use them. Lori Massad, head of human capital at AllianceBernstein, says she's been taken aside and chided for her four-inch-heel designer footwear, which one of her male colleagues had suggested was inappropriate. "It's a good thing I don't dress for you," she countered, explaining to me that the shoes made her feel "powerful and tall" and she wasn't about to give them up.

For men, as the Dukakis campaign discovered, there's not much to be done that doesn't risk exacerbating the image problem. (At one point, his handlers had Dukakis stand on a mound of earth behind a podium, but that only made the height disparity with Bush more apparent when he stepped off the mound.)[64] The best way to make height a nonissue is to take a page out of New York mayor Michael Bloomberg's playbook. Bloomberg's amour Diana Taylor, the former New York State superintendent of banks, is not only a good four inches taller but also inclined to appear by his side in showstopper heels. He "doesn't care" about their height difference, as he enjoys her looking good, Taylor told the *Huffington Post*.[65] A man secure enough to be photographed at the shoulder height of his girlfriend is a man no one will see as weak.

BEING YOUTHFUL AND VIGOROUS

Looking youthful, our survey respondents confirm, boosts the EP of both men and women because, like slimness and fitness,

it implies you've got the vitality to lead the charge and not suc-
cumb to setback. While anecdotal evidence suggests the band of
"age acceptability" for women is narrower than for men (a topic
we'll take up in the next chapter), the statistics on surgical interventions are impressive for both men and women. Like women,
men are shelling out on a staggering scale. Hair treatments are
a case in point, with men spending $1.8 billion a year on hair
implants and other treatments to prevent baldness. A full head
of hair for a man signals youth and vigor. (Consider that Ronald
Reagan's ample head of hair helped voters disregard the fact that,
at sixty-nine, he was the oldest president to take office.)[66] Both
men and women are also turning to plastic surgery as a solution
to ageism. Facelifts are up—126,000 in 2012, a 6 percent increase
from 2011—and Botox procedures continue to be the rage (6.1
million treatments in 2012, up 8 percent from 2011).[67] In fact, so
many men are opting for Botox injections that there's a slang term
for it: Brotox.[68] But the real stunner in terms of youth-enhancing
interventions for women is the "upper arm lift," a procedure that's
up 4,400 percent since 2000.[69]

As one who launched a new organization and a new career in
my fifties, I can affirm that nothing signals vitality in a middle-
aged woman more than toned arms with a discreet ripple of
muscle. My upper arms are pretty amazing—even if I do say so
myself (not quite up to Michelle Obama's standard, but close).
I'm a swimmer and relentless about my daily laps: It soothes my
soul as well as tones my body. So these days my professional wardrobe centers on slim-cut dresses—high-necked but bare-armed
(Michael Kors has a great selection). As the no-sleeve look isn't
always appropriate, I often team these dresses up with a well-
cut jacket or a graceful scarf. But it's the rare business event that
doesn't allow me to slip off my jacket, unsheathe those biceps, and
prove I'm up to the task before me.

If you cannot impress everyone with your obvious vitality, then at least make sure you minimize signs of age and downplay any infirmity. Consider how Franklin Delano Roosevelt managed his disability: Despite being neither young nor vital, he persuaded the world he was both, winning an unprecedented fourth term. Voters knew he'd been stricken with polio, and some Republicans tried to capitalize on it by suggesting that, as "a cripple," he was unfit for higher office.[70] Yet FDR, who established what became the March of Dimes during his presidency, "did not conceal his physical limitation except to prevent his opponents from making political capital out of it,"[71] enlisting the press to make sure photographs showed him standing unassisted. As a result, he was perceived as a leader who'd overcome disability to prevail—defeating formidable challenges.

The good news is that you don't need to ace all elements of appearance. If wearing high heels causes such toe-pinching agony that you can't deliver a dynamite presentation, then by all means wear flats and shift attention to your perfectly cut skirt or dress. The crucial point to keep in mind is that appearance is the medium for your message and, as such, it should neither distract nor detract from what you stand for and what you want to say.

## BLUNDERS

Avoiding appearance blunders (which oftentimes involves circumventing prejudice) is big—almost as important as nailing those five top appearance picks.

Provocative dressing tops the list of appearance blunders for women (see Figure 8). Senior men find an overtly sexual female colleague tantalizing and terrifying at the same time. And they have reason to be scared. Sex seems to addle the mind of accom-

plished, ambitious male leaders—they abandon reason and do stupid things (Anthony Weiner and Eliot Spitzer come to mind). Let's face it, nothing is more potentially career-ending for senior men than an illicit affair with a subordinate. Research conducted by CTI in 2010 reveals that illicit affairs—the actuality of one or the appearance of one—are toxic, as severe penalties accrue to both parties suspected of a dalliance. Fully 64 percent of senior male executives are hesitant to have one-on-one contact with high-performing junior women—out of fear, we infer, of fomenting perceptions that could lead to career derailment or even litigation. Hence the vehement reaction to blouses that feature cleavage, skirts that reveal a stretch of upper thigh, and knit dresses that cling to curvy bodies.

## Appearance Blunders

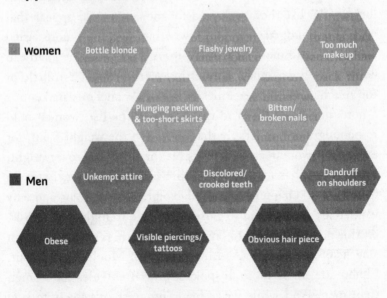

Figure 8. Appearance blunders

Looking unkempt in ways that aren't cool is the blunder that tops the list for men and comes in second for women. Fully 76 percent of senior executives say that being disheveled detracts from the EP of a man (rumpled jackets, ill-fitting collars, baggy or unbelted pants, scuffed shoes). In interviews they talked about how a disheveled appearance signals laziness and distracts attention. As one leader said, "Ketchup on a shirt or gravy on a tie catches the eye and makes it impossible to pay attention to more substantive qualities." So take pains to avoid looking sloppy and schlumpy—shine your shoes, retire blouses with underarm stains, repair fallen hems, take up too-long slacks, and iron your clothes. This will telegraph to those around you that you won't tolerate messiness in yourself or your work.

One distressing outcome: our survey respondents generated a list of appearance blunders for women that's literally twice as long as the list they generated for men. It would appear that women are judged, and found wanting, on many more visual attributes than men. Take makeup. A professional woman can commit an appearance blunder by wearing either too little or too much. For a man—unless he is a TV anchor—makeup is a nonissue. In addition to the length of the list, women tend to be judged more harshly than men. On the weight front, for example, a woman can be struck off the list if she's overweight, while a man has to be obese before he's passed over. Later on in this book (chapter 5) we shall explore in detail how and why women are scrutinized so closely and held to higher standards. At this point, suffice it to say that some of this critical attention smacks of gender bias. As Linda Huber of Moody's points out, "There are many more unspoken, unwritten rules for women than men. And while we've made progress, it's likely to stay that way."

## YOU'RE IN CONTROL

Long before her historic meeting with Mikhail Gorbachev in 1979, Margaret Thatcher, Britain's first and only female prime minister, demonstrated she was not a woman who would back down. Unwavering in her principles and unfazed by popular discontent, she'd emerged from Edward Heath's cabinet as a new kind of conservative, one who would champion individual empowerment over government intervention even as unemployment rose to record levels. So when the Soviets, hoping to denigrate her, dubbed her the Iron Lady, Thatcher immediately embraced the image publicly, as it paid tribute to both her steely resolve *and* her regal bearing. "I stand before you tonight in my Red Star chiffon evening gown, my face softly made up, and my fair hair gently waved, the Iron Lady of the Western World," she declared in a January 1976 speech to Conservatives in her home constituency of Finchley.[72] Clearly, she relished being seen as a leader of the free world who was both female and feminine *and* instilled fear and respect among strongmen opposed to everything she stood for.

And well she should have. Because Maggie Thatcher's image was one she carefully, consciously constructed. She worked on her look as assiduously as she worked on her voice. Long before anyone spoke of "image makeovers," Thatcher submitted to the ministrations of Gordon Reece, the television producer and marketing executive who'd brilliantly positioned her as an unthreatening homemaker during the "Margaret Thatcher, Milk Snatcher" days of austerity in the Heath cabinet, and then, just as brilliantly, sent her off to luxury clothier Aquascutum when she won the 1979 election. "Gordon was absolutely terrific," Thatcher revealed to her biographer. "He understood that it wasn't enough to have the right policies; one had to look good in putting them

over."[73] And she did. For Thatcher's visit to the Soviet Union, Marianne Abrahams, head of the venerable Aquascutum design team, outfitted her in tailored two-piece suits and seven "statement" coats—"a system that suited her on a daily basis so that she could be beautifully dressed and groomed and get on with running the country."[74]

The look that Thatcher adopted—the halo of hair, the large pearl jewelry, the bold and broad-shouldered suits, and the formidable handbag—proved so effective that other female leaders of the era were quick to follow (*Washington Post* publisher Katharine Graham was a dead ringer). U.S. diplomat Madeleine Albright picked up on (and made her signature) the large brooch on the lapel. Everywhere, big hair and shoulder pads recast women at work as more substantive players. Thatcher's black Launer handbags, which she tended to use as briefcases, influenced the size, color, and fashion of women's work accessories, not to mention how they used them to amplify their clout.

"She knew the importance of image from the very beginning," says Brenda Maddox, author of *Maggie: The First Lady*. "She had to put time into the way she dressed, but she got it right. She mastered power dressing before the phrase was even invented."[75]

This background on Thatcher underscores one final point: Image isn't inborn. Leaders create it, often with help. They diligently work to refine and maintain it. They take pains to avoid blunders that might destroy it.

And to be considered a leader, so must you.

## TACTICS

It's something of a final frontier, this business of appearance—not because others haven't probed it, but because so very few have

offered guidelines that might apply across the spectrum of workplace environments. There is, of course, no one "right" look. You must determine, by paying close attention to office culture cues and studying the leaders around you, what signals EP in your environment.

That said, from our deep tranche of qualitative research we can offer insights from individual managers across occupations and industries. At the minimum their stories and tips should prompt you to become conscious and therefore much more *intentional* about your appearance—a critical move toward acing it.

## SHOWCASE YOUR STRENGTHS

The stunning actress Olivia Wilde describes how, early in her career, she headed out for an audition wearing a huge cashmere turtleneck sweater over pants. Her boss stopped her at the door. "Olivia, what are you doing?" she cried. "You can't wear that! You have to wear something tight and sexy!" Wilde was taken aback: As a serious actress, confident in her craft, she wanted to focus her audience on her performance, not her physique. Her boss listened patiently, nodding in understanding, and then cut her off. "While I can appreciate you're not eager to sell yourself on pure sex appeal," she explained to Wilde, "it's ridiculous for someone with your curves to go into an audition hiding them. It signals a lack of awareness, even an immaturity on your part: This is a business that makes money by showcasing such assets." Wilde got it. She also won the audition.[76]

## SEEK PROFESSIONAL HELP

Go to a department store makeup counter and consult with the cosmetician. Hire a personal shopper. Consider hiring an image consultant. Paying for advice up front can save you a lot of money—and spare you some costly blunders.

IT'S NOT HOW GOOD YOU LOOK, IT'S HOW APPROPRIATE
YOU LOOK FOR YOUR AUDIENCE

A drug representative for Bristol-Myers Squibb described having
to send home a member of her team who showed up for a presentation at a Princeton, New Jersey, hospital wearing a sundress and
open-toed shoes. "We're meeting with people who are making
life-and-death decisions in there," the rep told this young woman.
"You can't hope to persuade them that you grasp the gravity of
their mission if you look like you're headed to a picnic." Reflecting
on this incident and others like it, this rep told me, "Too often, I
find, people just aren't thinking beyond themselves."

IF IT DOESN'T FEEL RIGHT, IT PROBABLY ISN'T

American Express's Kerrie Peraino advises women to listen to
"that little voice of anxiety" when it comes to vetting wardrobe
choices for work. "If I'm tugging at the back of my blouse all
day to keep the neckline from showing too much cleavage, then
clearly I'm not comfortable in that blouse—and won't derive a
lot of confidence from wearing it," she explains. She adds, "Your
work attire is your armor. It should make you feel invincible, not
add to your insecurities."

BEWARE OF CASUAL/COOL CULTURES

Last June, I was invited to keynote a session titled "Beyond Mad
Men" at the Cannes Lions Festival—the annual extravaganza of
the global advertising community. Michael Roth, the CEO of
Interpublic Group, wanted me to help him make the case that
Don Draper didn't cut the mustard these days—that the industry
needed more women at the top (only 3 percent of creative directors at the top fifty companies are female). I came through for
Roth—making a compelling case for why gender smarts mattered
for the bottom line. But brilliant presentation aside, I must admit

## Appearance

I was humbled by the visuals around me. This gathering of Mad Men (and a handful of Mad Women) showed the disadvantage women were at on the image front in a sector that is all about image. It's not that the "creatives" at this festival were drop-dead gorgeous—they were mature professionals in their forties and fifties and had their fair share of wrinkles and paunches. Rather, what was considered cool and chic was decidedly weighted in favor of men. The signature look of the rock stars of this advertising extravaganza comprised two-day-old stubble, bespoke shorts, and designer flip-flops. How does a woman—no matter how creative—bring this off?

This gender gap was painfully apparent at the awards ceremony. The men, blithely balding but sprouting impressive amounts of gray facial hair, looked suitably creative while still coming off as credible executives. The women, however, just looked wrong. Some played the formal card but ended up looking uncomfortable and straitjacketed in skirts and pantyhose; others played the expensive-casual game. It mostly backfired. Very few forty-five-year-women look like creative rock stars (or senior executives) in shorts and flip-flops—no matter how much they cost. They look as though they're heading to the beach. And as for facial hair . . .

### STAY IN COSTUME TO STAY IN CHARACTER

A colleague of mine describes how her boss leaves a suit jacket hanging on the back of his door in the event he's suddenly obliged to impress a client or superior. That's a flawed strategy, and here's why. First, you can't always know who among the people you encounter is worth impressing, nor can you always anticipate when and where you'll run into them. Second, gravitas isn't something you hang on the back of the door and wear at will. As we've discussed, a polished, well-put-together look is what communicates you're a person who is both respectful of

colleagues and clients and is yourself worthy of respect. Throwing on a jacket isn't likely to fool anyone. To *do* and *be* your best, you must strive to look your best, and that look depends on forethought and attention to detail. It's not an act so much as a mindset. Wear it when you walk in the office door and don't take it off until you're back home.

### DON'T LET YOUR BANGLES AND BLING STEAL YOUR THUNDER

Clanging, banging jewelry is not the best if you're giving a presentation, Linda Huber told me in an interview. "Anything that calls attention to itself rather than the message you're giving is not the best."

### WHEN IN DOUBT, LEAN ON YOUR SPONSOR

Trevor Phillips, former chair of Great Britain's Equality and Human Rights Commission, describes how he received an invitation from the deputy prime minister to Chevening, the stately country retreat shared by the deputy prime minister and the foreign secretary (akin to getting invited to Camp David by an American president). His fiancée, a graduate of Cambridge, asked him what he thought she should wear. Phillips shrugged off her concern. "Don't be stupid," she persisted. "Find out what I am supposed to wear." So Phillips put a call into the deputy prime minister's secretary, who assured him there was no dress code—guidance he duly passed along to his wife-to-be. "You're an idiot," she told him. "'No dress code' means, if you don't know the code, you shouldn't be there." Phillips, a London native of Afro-Caribbean descent, turned to his sponsor for guidance. "If, like me, you're an outsider to these circles, it's essential you consult someone who not only can help you crack the code, but whose vested interest in you will prompt them to do so," he says.

# Appearance

### ASK FOR SPECIFIC FEEDBACK—AND SIGNAL THAT YOU'RE OKAY WITH UNVARNISHED CRITICISM

Giving pointers to someone else about his or her appearance is daunting and difficult, which is why you see so many blunders on parade by people who should know better (we'll discuss feedback failures in chapter 5). So make it easier: Ask your superiors for feedback on your attire, hairstyle, and grooming. Provide assurance that you will receive their observations and suggestions not as fault-finding but as constructive guidance, and dig deep to ensure you understand how to correct your gaffes. Live up to your promise by listening rather than reacting defensively. While it will be painful to hear what you're doing wrong, consider how much more painful it is to learn about your blunders later, from someone else, when it's too late to reverse first impressions.

### BUY YOURSELF GREATER LATITUDE

Executive presence is all about inspiring trust and confidence in others. Once you've done that and are successfully "over the bar," you can start to play with the dress code; ultimately you get to set the dress code. Steve Jobs, let it be said, didn't start out with fifty black turtlenecks: That signature look (thinking different, dressing different) evolved in lockstep with his extraordinary success. In the battle between conformity and authenticity, *you* will eventually prevail—not, perhaps, as a brand-new hire but down the road when you have some seniority. Get over the bar. Establish your bona fides. Win everyone's faith and confidence. Then make your own rules.

# 5

When Aileen, an executive at a pharmaceutical firm, assumed leadership of its global medical division, she conducted a review of her U.S.-based staff that included 360s, performance evaluations, and one-on-one assessments. As the December holidays approached, she met with all of her direct reports to share what she had learned and discuss either their opportunities to advance or the gaps they needed to close. The meetings went well: Aileen's assessments aligned with feedback her direct reports had already received. But at one meeting, an African-American woman who'd been assured of a promotion by Aileen's predecessor took exception to the news that she had neither the skills nor the leadership presence to qualify for a higher role. Not only did she take exception, but she threatened to quit on the spot.

Alarmed and concerned, Aileen urged her to take some time over the holiday break to think about her next steps and come back to her in the New Year to discuss a plan. "Quite honestly, I was terrified we were veering into EEOC territory," recalls Aileen, referring to the federal Equal Employment Opportunity Commission. "I was prepared to stand by my assessment but wanted time to review it with legal before meeting with her again."

In January, they reconvened in Aileen's office. "I've done some careful thinking," the woman began. "I realized over Christmas that, in all the years I've worked for this firm, not one person has

taken issue with my performance or questioned my leadership capabilities. When I've asked for constructive criticism on my presentations, everyone has told me I'm doing just fine. In fact, I've been handed every promotion I've asked for—up until recently, when you arrived."

The woman paused. Aileen held her breath.

"If you would work with me," she continued, "I would very much like to work with you to develop myself as a leader and get to the next level."

With that meeting began an extraordinary alliance. "I talked her up to colleagues who could pull her onto teams where she could get the client exposure and training she needed," Aileen told me. "And she was fiercely loyal to me throughout my own transition here. Today, she's heading up our marketing team."

## WHY FEEDBACK FAILS

Think for a minute: When's the last time someone at work gave you honest, critical feedback on some aspect of your EP?

For that matter, when's the last time you *gave* someone at work a critical and specific EP pointer?

Unvarnished, concrete feedback on your appearance, communication skills, and gravitas is hard to come by. It's especially hard if you're female, though your chances improve slightly with a same-sex boss.

It's not hard to see why. Consider the situation Joe Stringer, a partner in EY in London, found himself in when a client told him that they had concerns about the appearance of one of the female members of his project team. Curvy, blond, and inclined to wear inappropriate blouses and short skirts, the woman didn't exude the professionalism, the client told Stringer, that he ex-

pected of an EY employee. "The trolley-dolly image doesn't help," the client added. But Stringer couldn't bring himself to confront his team member about her distracting attire. "I couldn't think of a way to point out what was wrong without sounding like I was noticing all the wrong things about her," he explains. He did, however, enlist her in a development course on client interaction, where she was able to make the connection between image and impact and set about transforming herself. "She's a different person now, a real rising star on the team," notes Stringer. He adds, "Thankfully it worked its way through, but if I'd been confident enough to say something, it might have happened more quickly."

This story goes to show not only how EP feedback can make a critical difference in a woman's career but also why women often don't get it from their (male) superiors. Senior men just can't afford to have their motives misconstrued. Consider the illustrious list of now-deposed CEOs who've had to step down because of improper dealings with female subordinates. Whatever the true nature of their interactions, it takes only the perception that something unprofessional has transpired to bring down the mighty. For example, Mark Hurd, former CEO of Hewlett-Packard, was called to account by the board for fudging his expense sheet—merely for attempting to hide, not have, extracurricular encounters with HP subcontractor Jodie Fisher.

As every male who's been subjected to sexual-harassment training might conclude, developing female talent by giving women individualized feedback just isn't worth the added risk of bumping against the third rail of office politics. Indeed, that risk effectively keeps men from helping women develop and advance as leaders, which helps explain why the marzipan layer is thick with highly qualified women (34 percent of senior managers are now female, according to CTI research) while the executive band remains thinly populated (14.3 percent of executives are female).[77]

Giving critical EP feedback—one of the key roles an effective sponsor plays—is just so much easier man-to-man. Men will alert other men to wince-inducing EP gaffes such as bad breath or an unzipped fly, but confronted with a woman in too short a skirt or too tight a top, they'll look away. Better to stay mum about a woman's inappropriate attire than be sued for noticing it.

For similar reasons, people of color don't get the feedback they need to develop their EP: Fearing discomfort as well as discrimination litigation, senior executives told us they would sooner pass over multicultural professionals lacking executive presence than have an honest conversation about their shortcomings. In particular, people of color don't get unvarnished feedback about hair, clothing, and body weight, according to our survey results. Participants in our focus groups all had a story to share about tripping over the race issue in giving and getting critical feedback on EP, most particularly when it comes to deficits on communication skills and presentation of self. One Asian executive spoke to me of how she inadvertently unleashed a discrimination suit when she critiqued a Hispanic woman on her team for her shortcomings in failing to prepare adequately for a presentation. Her team member accused her of "fomenting and tolerating a workplace culture that was hostile to Latinas," citing snubs and slights that surfaced bias around Latinas' work ethic and emotional temperament. "It was an outrageous claim, given that the head of our division is part Puerto Rican," this Asian executive explained. "But I've seen it too many times to dismiss it: Nine times out of ten, the aggrieved party will pull the race card. And then the whole workplace takes a step backward, in terms of diversity, because after a messy and costly dismissal every leader privately concludes 'That's the last time I'll hire a fill-in-the-blank.'" She added, "I know we'll have reached real equality when people of color get fired as easily as white people."

People of color likewise spoke of the damage they've suffered—in lost opportunities, mostly, but also in terms of their
self-esteem—as a result of white people's perceptions that they'll
go nuclear if they're found wanting in any way. As an African-
American partner with Deloitte Consulting explains, the insin-
uation underlying feedback that's restrained or outright withheld
is that you're someone "who is actually incapable of hurdling the
bar others are held to."

## DIFFICULT CONVERSATIONS—BUT
## EXTRAORDINARILY IMPORTANT

It must be said that some kinds of feedback are intrinsically difficult to give no matter who is on the receiving end. Criticizing
someone's appearance, for example, turns out to be emotionally
fraught, even woman-to-woman. "You're taking issue with their
self-expression," Rohini Anand, global diversity officer for Sodexo, points out. "How can that not be taken personally?"

Indeed, our survey data reveals that, when it comes to appearance, women can be harsher judges of other women than are
men. They're more likely than men to consider "poorly maintained clothing" an EP blunder for women, and more likely to
dock women EP points for wearing too-tight clothing.

Correcting someone on how they speak is also dicey terrain,
even when that speech pattern is affecting business outcomes and
limiting personal career trajectories. That's because, like appearance, taking issue with grammar, accent, or diction goes straight
to ethnic, cultural, or socioeconomic differences.

"I give lots of presentation pointers," says Anand, "but I truly
hesitate when it comes to correcting someone on their diction unless we have a genuinely trusting relationship." (Recall Katherine

# Female Appearance Blunders

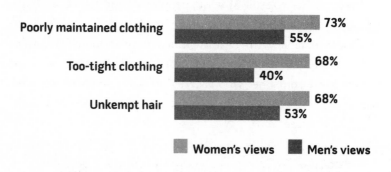

Poorly maintained clothing — Women's views 73%, Men's views 55%

Too-tight clothing — Women's views 68%, Men's views 40%

Unkempt hair — Women's views 68%, Men's views 53%

Women's views    Men's views

---

**Figure 9. Female appearance blunders**

Phillips's story in chapter 3 about her thesis advisor correcting her pronunciation of "aks" to "ask"—a bold move indeed.)

Overwhelmingly, however, the consensus among our interviewees is that dispensing good critical feedback across all three EP pillars is a core leadership competency, one that should be developed and evaluated along with other managerial skills. Women and people of color I interviewed who'd been on the receiving end of good EP feedback were adamant about this, as the impact on their own careers had been profound. Receiving such feedback, they acknowledge, can feel like undergoing root canal surgery: Christina, a communications executive, tells of being "stung to her core" when told that her male subordinate had been mistaken for her superior in a meeting because he exuded more leadership presence than she did. And to be sure, giving EP pointers is no picnic: Annalisa Jenkins, global head of research and development at Merck Serono, has more than once reduced women to tears when delivering constructive criticism. But to shirk the

imperative of giving feedback on leadership presence is to throw into question your standing as a leader. "Leadership isn't about being voted Ms. Popular," says Sodexo's Anand. "To be effective, it's more important to be honest, and have those courageous conversations, than to be liked. At the end, that is what will garner the trust and respect so crucial to leadership."

I spoke to one high-flying consultant who actually quit a lucrative job at a bank because she couldn't get her superiors to have those conversations with her. Whenever she asked for explicit feedback on how she handled a presentation or a client encounter, she was told she didn't need any. "You're doing great!" her boss assured her. She attributes this cop-out to two things: an absence of regular, formalized assessments in her division, even though the tools existed, and a lack of leadership sensibilities among the financial service managers to whom she reported. "They were dealmakers, people who got promoted for hitting the numbers and making money," she explains. "I wasn't impressed with them. They had nothing to teach me, and I wouldn't have wanted to go anywhere they were headed. To develop my own leadership capabilities, I had to leave."

## WHAT GREAT FEEDBACK SOUNDS LIKE

If giving EP feedback marks you as a leader, then giving actionable EP feedback marks you as a great one. From our interviews, consensus emerged on what constitutes truly constructive criticism. A few examples:

- Poised to go into a meeting with someone who reported directly to her CEO, newly promoted Christina was asked to stop by her new boss's office

first. "Your extensive knowledge of the business will earn you credibility," the woman told Christina, smiling to reassure her. "But I notice when you're nervous you talk fast, and that can come across as junior. Take a deep breath. Take a moment to adjust to your audience. Don't be afraid to create some silence."

■ On returning from a conference, Tara, a new addition to Rohini Anand's team at Sodexo, got this feedback from Anand's colleague on how to better represent the company: "Look, this job requires a lot of networking. I see, when I take you to events, that you're not mingling except with people on your team. I want you to come back from these gatherings with a stack of business cards. I want you to forge at least five new relationships, and follow up on each of them, because as a senior member of this team it's important that potential clients know you personally."

■ "With this particular leader, you've got to cut a very different image or you're going to get cut from his team," one chief learning officer recalls hearing from his boss when he was a new hire at a financial services corporation. "This leader values precision and attention to detail, and in your manner and style of dress you're not convincing him that you, too, value these things. Be on time for meetings, not five minutes late. Put in more effort and energy preparing your presentation. And your wardrobe has to be a cut above. The suit you're wearing is inappropriate. You need better shirts and better shoes, and if you'd like I can tell you three places to find them."

Ear-burning stuff, yes? But consider, after the shock wears off, what you will have learned from the leader who delivers such feedback:

- ✓ *You'll be clear on what the problem is.*
- ✓ *You'll understand why it must be addressed.*
- ✓ *You'll know precisely what you need to do to course-correct.*

In short, we know from our qualitative data that great feedback is (1) timely, meaning it's delivered either right before or right after you've blundered; (2) specific to one discrete behavior, as opposed to a global condemnation; and (3) prescriptive, or explicit about what actions need to be taken by you. It should also be framed in the context of the business outcome, whether that outcome is your personal success (for example, exuding gravitas at an important meeting with a superior) or the success of your team (for example, holding on to key clients). There are of course endless variations that nuance this formula, but in essence you follow these guidelines.

All of this makes perfect sense when you consider our survey results on what characterizes *bad* feedback. Feedback is bad when it sets up a very narrow band of acceptability, a phenomenon we'll explore at length in the next chapter: Women, for example, are told they're either too angry or too nice, overly passive or way too aggressive, too young or too old. They're told they need to "dial it back" or "step up to the plate," "rein in the emotion" or "show some humanity." Feedback is bad, too, when it's vague: Carolyn Buck Luce, a former head of the global health care practice at EY, recalls being told as a senior executive that she needed to become "more vulnerable." What was she supposed to do with this comment? Given the ubiquity of bad feedback in the workplace, it comes as no surprise that the majority of our respondents say they haven't been able to act on the feedback they've been given.

Improving feedback will require a two-pronged approach. First, you as a rising star must learn to become better at eliciting, receiving, and acting on criticism. And second, you as a leader must become better at giving criticism while still modeling how to receive it.

## TACTICS: HOW TO GET THE EP FEEDBACK YOU NEED

### RECOGNIZE YOU NEED IT

In her twenties, as the newly appointed sales manager at a telephone directory printing firm, Debbie Storey was asked to present her business plan for the coming year. "I'd never created one, let alone seen one delivered," she recalls. But she had lots of ideas—and felt compelled to share them all in her ten-minute slot. "The longer I spoke, the more I realized I had *way* too much material," Storey recalls. "People were squirming in their seats. I saw my boss's face fall, I saw the look of horror on the president's face." After the meeting, Storey sought out her boss and asked for training in public speaking. "No one needed to tell me I had bombed," she says. "I knew I needed help." Not everybody, however, recognizes they do. On the contrary, says communications exec Christina, "everybody says they welcome feedback, but then persists in thinking they're perfect." She adds, "People I know, probably the smartest people in my group, won't be going anywhere because they don't have EP. And they don't have EP because they don't accept that they need to acquire it."

### DEVELOP A THICKER SKIN

Debora Spar, president of Barnard College, distinguished herself early among a circle of outstanding peers at Harvard University

by putting herself repeatedly in the line of fire that emanated from her graduate advisors. "The biggest compliment one of them ever paid me was 'Not bad,'" she says. "But I'd go back for more, because I knew I had a lot to learn." The more Spar demonstrated she could take the heat, the bigger the kitchen she was asked to run. "I'm grateful to have been raised by wolves," she says. "I don't need that pat on the head to excel. I think we're raising both women and men to be overly sensitive to criticism, so that when they finally get out in the real world and they don't get a 5.0 on a performance review, they fall apart. It's so important, early in life, to get that lesson and toughen up."

## ROUTINELY ASK FOR SPECIFIC, TIMELY, PRESCRIPTIVE FEEDBACK

If you make a blanket request, as in "How am I doing?," you may get a blanket answer ("Just fine!"). Better to laser in on a recent encounter that required considerable EP—a meeting with a high-powered client or leader in the firm—and request that a superior assess you on your body language, speech and delivery, attire, command of the room, and so on. The assessment itself needn't take place immediately, but your request for it should. And if nothing happens, ask again. "Say, 'It's been a while, I'd really like some pointed feedback from you,'" suggests Lisa Garcia Quiroz, head of corporate social responsibility for Time Warner. "Then put on your iron panties."

## IF YOU CAN'T GET ACTIONABLE FEEDBACK FROM YOUR SUPERIORS, ASK FOR A COACH—OR PAY OUT-OF-POCKET YOURSELF

Far from betraying a lack of EP, asking for professional help (if need be on your own dime), signals a considerable level of personal maturity and professional commitment. In some

organizations this leadership perk is conferred on "high potentials." Whoever pays for the executive coach, he/she can help you with your image (wardrobe and hair styling), presentation skills, and overall gravitas—even when you think you've already got a leg up on other people and don't need much help. Elizabeth, a retail products executive, worked with an executive coach when she transitioned from a consulting firm to a corporate environment, a process she found eye-opening because she thought she'd learned everything she needed to know working for McKinsey. Through videotaped sessions, she says, she learned to modulate her style to fit her new environment: doing more listening than talking, speaking slower instead of selling ideas in a rapid-fire style. "You think you don't use ums and ahs, you think your expression is under control, you think you're concise and hard-hitting," she says. "It's hard to see yourself on video, as others see you, but until you do, you'll never face facts."

## CREATE A CIRCLE OF PEERS WITH WHOM YOU CAN SHARE FEEDBACK

Relentless in her desire to improve, Elizabeth also seeks out feedback from both men and women she has come to know and trust—a two-way exchange on what's working and not working that occurs all day, every day. "If a peer asks for an opinion, I'm going to be honest, because I'd expect the same of her or him," she notes. "It comes down to trust." Trust, in turn, is built on a foundation of shared lunches, cups of coffee, drinks after work, or extracurricular activities around charity, sports, or kids, Elizabeth explains. "I always find the time to reach out to people on my team and build these relationships," she says. "I will make sure I'm there to support them when they need my feedback, because at some point I'm going to need theirs."

### TURN TO MENTORS

Feeling stalled in her career, Sylvie, a budget analyst working in television, turned to the National Black MBA Association for mentoring help. The female executive assigned to her took one appraising look at her and shook her head. "If you want to advance, you're going to have to do something about your appearance," the executive told her. "You look like a little kid, and people are not going to trust a little kid to do a grown-up's job." She suggested Sylvie get her hair cut and styled, wear more makeup, and upgrade her attire, advice that Sylvie promptly acted on. Within less than three months, she was given oversight of a new hire and a major stretch assignment. Today, she is a senior analyst at her mentor's firm.

### CULTIVATE A SPONSOR

Sponsors are not mentors. Sponsors are powerful leaders who see potential in you and, provided you give them 110 percent, will go out on a limb to make things happen for you. Because sponsors have a vested interest in how you turn out (your reputation now being linked with their own), they will give you the kind of feedback that mentors can't or won't. Tim Melville-Ross, formerly CEO of Nationwide (as I mentioned earlier, the biggest building society in the United Kingdom, equivalent to a U.S. savings-and-loan institution), describes how one of the nonexecutive directors on the board sponsored him in his candidacy for the role of chief executive officer—by telling him what he could not otherwise have known about his standing in the race. "You are very agreeable and well liked, and others enjoy your humor," Melville-Ross was told, "but we need to see your challenging side in the boardroom." How to do that? "Pick the most senior nonexecutive member of the board"—the director named the member—"and pick a fight with him. Make a challenging remark. Point out

something as absolute rubbish." Melville-Ross did precisely that, provoking horror around the table. But a good kind of horror, he says. "When I looked at the director, who was sitting next to this member I'd just attacked," Melville-Ross recalls, "he gave me an enormous wink."

### LISTEN FOR THE "RING OF TRUTH"

Not all feedback is accurate or well-intentioned, and occasionally you will be the recipient of off-base, ill-timed, vague feedback. But don't dismiss it out of hand. As Suzi Digby, the British choral conductor, told me, there's no such thing as a bad review—not if you tune your radar for that ping that can help you course-correct. "I've had good reviews and the odd negative one. The reviewer is not always right, but sometimes you recognize the ring of truth in a critical comment, and it's important to allow it to be processed."

### DEMONSTRATE YOU WILL ACT ON THE FEEDBACK YOU'VE BEEN GIVEN

It's one thing to nod agreeably to constructive criticism; it's quite another to change your behavior as a result. Yet unless you show superiors that you are willing to course-correct, they might conclude you're not worth the time and energy it takes to impart difficult feedback in the first place. Rohini Anand suggests getting a reality check if you're hesitating to act, as sometimes hearing criticism from peers as well as superiors can bring your next action into sharper focus. With one boss, the feedback Anand received was somewhat oblique: "When I come in with something at a later phase, your mind is already made up," he told her. Only when she got the results of a 360, which pointed out that she tended not to consistently allow other ideas to bubble up and gain traction, did Anand understand she needed to do a better job at

listening to and eliciting late-stage innovations from her team. "I now hold my comments and views until I've heard from everybody," she says. "I want to be sure I model receptivity."

## WHEN YOU'RE GIVEN VAGUE CRITICISM, GET CLARITY BY ASKING HOW YOUR BEHAVIOR IS NEGATIVELY IMPACTING OUTCOMES

When feedback is confusing, says Carolyn Buck Luce, it's almost inevitably a symptom of cultural misalignment. "You need to be more vulnerable" was her manager's way of saying, she realized, "Your personal style is clashing with the culture of this organization." To better understand that clash, Buck Luce asked her boss, "How is what I'm doing getting in the way of my job?" Her manager explained that, by never asking for help and not explaining to others what she was doing, Buck Luce was inadvertently signaling that (1) her agenda was more important than theirs and (2) she didn't value other perspectives. "That made a lot of sense," she says. "I realized I wasn't forging enough strategic alliances, that to be effective at a more senior level, I needed to widen my pool of go-to people." She adds, "Women take this sort of thing personally, but they need to realize, when your manager asks you to change, it's not because there's something wrong with you: It's the culture crying!"

## DON'T BURST INTO TEARS

Of course criticism hurts. And yes, you're going to take it personally because some of it is directed at you personally. But put on your best face with your critics, and save your tears for later, because nothing cuts off the spigot of vital feedback more effectively than a loss of emotional control. "Try and remember this is a learning opportunity," advises Time Warner's Lisa Garcia Quiroz. "You have a responsibility to listen, and react appropri-

ately, just as your manager has a responsibility to deliver his or her insight. If you sit there and get angry or emotional, then it will be so much tougher for the two of you to have subsequent conversations. Your manager may feel it's a waste of time, or conclude you're incapable of growing. And then it becomes a self-fulfilling prophecy: If you don't get feedback, you cannot grow."

### NEVER BURN A BRIDGE

You may decide, upon hearing negative or critical feedback, that it's time to seek a job elsewhere. This does not entitle you to unleash your anger or give a vindictive response, cautions Garcia Quiroz. Rather, concede the point and show you're interested in preserving everybody's well-being. Work with your manager to have a seamless and mature transition. You need him or her to be supportive of your transition and may even need a recommendation to secure your next opportunity. Be proactive and honest if you know this is not a work situation that you can turn around. "What's important," says Garcia Quiroz, "is that you show you're going to take responsibility for your career—by managing the terms of your own exit."

## TACTICS: HOW TO GIVE EP FEEDBACK LIKE A TRUE LEADER

### GIVE FREQUENT, DISCRETE POINTERS RATHER THAN SEMI-ANNUAL DOWNLOADS

If by the time you sit down to impart feedback you've accumulated a laundry list of criticisms, then you've waited too long. Criticism cannot be constructive when it's too lengthy. Inventorying someone's shortcomings in one sitting is more likely to paralyze or demoralize than incentivize that person to change.

## DON'T IMPART FEEDBACK WHEN YOU'RE ANGRY

Wait twenty-four hours, or until you've cooled down, before calling someone to account for a massive blunder. You'll both have gained much-needed perspective on what happened. If you give feedback in the heat of the moment, observes Garcia Quiroz, you risk exposing yourself as someone not in control of your game—and that lapse in leaderlike behavior gives your subordinate license to shift more of the blame to you. "People will blame everybody except themselves when they're hurt or angry," she observes. "For criticism to be constructive, it has to be delivered without the emotion that signals 'personal attack.'"

## PUT THE GOOD THINGS OUT THERE FIRST

Recognize what people have achieved or are achieving before pointing out what they haven't delivered. You'll appear to be a more credible critic, one worth heeding, if you demonstrate you've observed the good in measure equal to the bad. Communications exec Christina says she always starts a feedback session by soliciting the other person's self-assessment first. "Tell me the three areas where you think you're doing great," she opens. "Then tell me the three areas where you want to improve."

## EMBED CORRECTIVES IN YOUR CRITICISM

In a postmortem with one of her personnel trainers, AT&T's Debbie Storey detailed not just those aspects of the woman's delivery that needed improvement but also those actions that might improve her delivery. Storey had observed that this trainer lost her audience before she ever won them, first by jumping right into the material and then by talking very fast in a low monotone. So she couched her feedback in what to do, rather than what to stop doing. "Think about how to get the audience with you before launching into the content," she began. "Let them get to know

you, and understand where you're going, before you go there. Then help them keep up: Talk more slowly. Pause more often. Try to inject humor, because this material is dry by nature and you're funny by nature. Let people see there's more to you than dry content, and they'll come back for more."

CATCH PEOPLE WHEN THEY'RE GETTING IT RIGHT

Especially when the wisdom you're trying to impart concerns a person's appearance, pounce on any opportunity to congratulate that person for having made good choices. Christina describes one woman whose "completely showstopping, inappropriate attire" had caught the eye of everyone in management, but whom no one had confronted. Watching her manager struggle over this, Christina waited until this woman arrived one day dressed more appropriately and then pulled her into her office to rave about her appearance. "This is a wonderful look for you, a really good look for you as a career professional," Christina gushed. It worked: Overnight, says Christina, the woman seemingly bought new clothes to continue eliciting Christina's praise. "You want to think about the outcome before you pull someone into your office and say, 'I can see through your dress.' Nobody is going to feel good about that conversation."

PREFACE FEEDBACK WITH THE ASSURANCE THAT YOU HAVE THAT PERSON'S BEST INTERESTS AT HEART AND WISH TO ENSURE THEIR SUCCESS

"This may not be easy to hear," Rohini Anand will begin by saying, "but please depersonalize it. I'm telling you this because I want you to be successful." Better yet, if you're that person's sponsor, establish the ground rules for feedback before you deliver any. Kent Gardiner, chair of Crowell & Moring, "struck a deal" with an African-American attorney in whom he saw great promise. He

asked him if he wanted feedback on his courtroom manner and style of delivery. Assured that he did, Gardiner further asked if he'd be willing to hear criticism from the chairman of the firm in the spirit in which it was intended, in other words, as an EP tip and not a threat to his standing in the firm. "Feedback works only if there's mutual trust and respect," says Gardiner. "Our agreement assured him that I had his best interests at heart, and he assured me he could listen to what I had to say without taking offense."

## DISCUSS APPEARANCE IN THE CONTEXT OF PERSONAL BRANDING

Storey situates any comments she may have about an employee's wardrobe choices in a larger conversation about that employee's personal brand. "Help them identify that brand first," Storey says. "Then you can afford to point out how their personal style may clash or support that image." For example, talk about their skills and passions, and discuss what distinctive value they add to the team, as in 'You're known for your analytical skills, and your ability to see the trend behind the numbers.' Then stress how every interaction, every verbal and nonverbal message they send, including their clothing and overall appearance, should serve to reinforce that image."

## ENLIST A THIRD PARTY

If you're concerned in the least that your feedback might be misconstrued as discrimination, share your concerns with an HR or diversity specialist. That third party might refer you to legal counsel, or counsel you directly on ways to handle the conversation so that it doesn't veer into EEOC territory. At the very least, you may find it helpful to role-play with a trained professional to ensure that feedback is received as constructively—and nonlitigiously—as possible.

Good feedback on executive presence is hard to come by—it's difficult to give, difficult to elicit, and difficult to receive. The issue is even more sensitive for women, people of color, and LGBT employees. The good news is that improving the feedback loop is a central part of EP workshops and training sessions that have been developed by CTI over the last two years.[i]

---

[i] For more information, see Center for Talent Innovation at www.talentinnovation.org and Hewlett Consulting Partners at www.hewlettconsultingpartners.com.

# 6

For as long as Hillary Clinton has been part of the zeitgeist—as first lady, as senator, as presidential candidate, and as secretary of state—she has been pilloried for failing to be all things to all people. Too female to be taken seriously (remember that bit of cleavage she revealed on the Senate floor?), she was at the same time considered too aggressive to be considered appropriately feminine (driving health-care reform was seen as unseemly and un-first-lady-like). She was too accomplished to appeal to the electorate (C-student George W. Bush having set the bar) but too politically inexperienced to be seen as "electable." She was perceived as too much "Bill's wife" to run for office, but not enough of a mother to Chelsea (too few cookies baked) to win the women's vote. To her enormous credit, Hillary persevered in the face of this whiplash, garnering for herself as secretary of state global as well as national respect. But that hasn't liberated her from the high-wire act she's walked as a woman seeking higher office. She is still too female to be "presidential material"—yet somehow at the same time seen as too masculine to appeal to voters. In the court of public opinion Hillary just can't win.

## A NARROW BAND OF ACCEPTABILITY

Carolyn Buck Luce, a leader who has negotiated narrow bands of acceptability for decades, calls this the Goldilocks syndrome. "You're never 'just right,'" she explains. "You're too this, you're too that—and you always will be, because what's behind it is hidden bias. If you don't fit the stereotype of a leader, you're not likely to be seen as becoming one."

If you're not straight, or not white, or not male, that is, and you aspire to leadership, you're likely to find yourself up against the impossible expectation that you be someone you're intrinsically not. This expectation is communicated via feedback that's inherently contradictory or paradoxical, and that so many on the path to leadership have had to parse before they can proceed. Consider the impossible demands that met Barack Obama on his first presidential run: He was "too white" for black voters,[78] but "too black" for white voters.[79]

Hillary is also a standout example of the Goldilocks syndrome—but many less illustrious women struggle with the perception that they are either too much or too little, never just right. The majority of women being considered as potential "leadership material" hover in that layer just below top management, what's known as the marzipan layer because it's so rich with talent—and so sticky. Women comprise today more than half of the highly qualified talent pipeline (holding some 60 percent of graduate degrees), and the majority (64 percent of senior women, according to CTI research) are eager to be promoted to the next job level.[80] Yet we also find that, at the door to the C-suite, they hesitate to cross the threshold—fearful, we suspect, of having to walk the tightrope between feminine and authoritative, and between effective and likable. Men simply aren't forced to

choose, since by dint of being male they're already perceived as leadership material. Since the early 1970s, when social scientist Virginia Schein showed that both male and female managers perceive leadership attributes as more likely to be held by men than by women, studies have repeatedly confirmed that we associate masculine attributes with leadership suitability and feminine attributes with serve-ability—"taking charge" skills being the province of men, and "taking care" skills being the province of women.[81] Despite research showing that gender is not a reliable predictor of how a person will lead, we persist in vetting leadership candidates on precisely that basis.[82] Women are seen to embody such "feminine" traits as being less self-confident, less analytical, and less emotionally stable, traits not associated with capable leaders; whereas traits we associate with being masculine—being aggressive, dominant, objective, and competitive—are considered requisite to leadership.[83] Compounding this stereotypical perception of women is men's inability to perceive their own "invisible knapsack" of privilege, that kit of inborn traits that grants them access, acceptance, and authority they don't even realize they have and are carrying.[84]

When women do manifest the requisite traits, we're inclined to punish them for it. Experiments repeatedly surface our inclination to fault women for career ambition and entrepreneurial smarts while rewarding it in men. In an experiment conducted at the Stern School of Business at New York University in 2003, male and female graduate students who assessed the leadership capabilities of a real-life successful entrepreneur named Heidi were far more inclined to admire this accomplished individual when she was recast as Howard. Students given the case study about Heidi perceived her as "selfish," "out for herself," and "a little political"—in short, not as likable as Howard. When this experiment was replayed in 2013, substituting Kathryn and Martin for

Heidi and Howard, students actually liked Kathryn slightly better than Martin (8.0 versus 7.6)—but they didn't *trust* her nearly as much (6.4 for Kathryn, 7.8 for Martin). As the evaluators explained to CNN correspondent Anderson Cooper, who staged the replay, "men seem more genuine," whereas women seem to be "trying too hard," making them less trustworthy.[85]

The likability-versus-competence trade-off is arguably the most tenacious, as well as pernicious, double bind that women in leadership confront. First documented in 2004, when Madeline Heilman and others found that successful women, unlike successful men, suffered social rejection and personal derogation (especially when their success was in a male-dominated arena),[86] it continues to be corroborated. A large-scale study of 60,470 men and women conducted in 2011 found that, while slightly more than half (54 percent) of participants said they had no preference when it came to choosing the gender of their boss, the other 46 percent indicated a strong preference for a male superior—by more than a 2-to-1 ratio, in fact. Those who said they preferred a male boss cited not the positive attributes of male leaders, but rather the negative attributes of female leaders. Comments such as "catty" or "bitchy" cropped up a lot in these discussions. "While not directly addressing the competence of female leaders, these comments attach the personality of the female leader, indicating that some perceive these abstract female leaders as less likeable than men," the researchers observed.[87]

Every time a woman takes the national or international stage, the likability/effectiveness double bind surfaces. When Michelle Bachelet became Chile's first female president in 2006, detractors didn't waste time in taking her to task for being overly "female" in her approach. "She makes commissions," her opponents said, dismissively, "not decisions."[88] She was also referred to as La Gordis ("Fatty"), something that describes Chris Christie but has never

been thrown at him in the press. Bachelet was at once "too maternal" (as an inclusive leader who listened to others' input and sought consensus) and "too tough" (she was, after all a survivor of torture under Pinochet and the country's first female defense minister in 2002).[89]

Eventually Bachelet proved that a female leader could be both effective *and* endearing: She left office with approval ratings of 84 percent,[90] preparing her for a second run as an opposition candidate in 2013. But other high-flying females, according to those who track them, have had to choose. "Women can be powerful. Women can be likeable. Being both is difficult to do," observed Patricia Sellers, the compiler of *Fortune*'s most-powerful-women list.[91] Feminist blogger Jessica Valenti, writing for the *Nation*, noted that "women adjust their behavior to be likeable and as a result have less power in the world"—an acceptable trade-off, to her way of thinking, but nonetheless a trade-off.[92] Most recently, Sheryl Sandberg, Facebook's number two, has observed the trade-off and lamented its impact on potentially high-impact women. "I believe this bias is at the very core of why women hold themselves back," she wrote in her 2013 take-charge manifesto, *Lean In*. "It is also at the very core of why women are held back."[93]

## NO BANDWIDTH

Has nothing changed? Are women indeed "damned if they do, doomed if they don't"?[94]

Data from CTI's survey research suggests the band of acceptability for women leaders hasn't widened much in the decades since Virginia Schein documented the "think leader, think male" conflation. Across all three pillars of executive presence—gravitas, communication, and appearance—women continue to walk a tightrope.

## The Fine Line of Executive Presence
Female leaders have little latitude

Figure 10. The fine line of executive presence

## APPEARANCE

Looking like a leader, for women, turns out to be terrain studded with land mines. We found that, while women are as likely as men to believe appearance plays a small part in a leader's executive presence, women are much more likely to be pilloried on the basis of it, whatever they do. Focus group participants told us, for example, that too much makeup undermines a woman's credibility—but then faulted female leaders for looking too frumpy or unpolished (citing, of course, Hillary Clinton). Almost half of our survey respondents said that unkempt nails detract from a woman's EP, yet nearly as many said that "overly done"

nails were unleaderlike. The issue of age, which hardly comes up for men, is fraught with peril for women: Almost the same number of respondents said "looking too young" was a liability as told us "looking too old" undermined a woman's EP. When we pressed managers to identify for us the "sweet spot" for women in terms of looking just the right age, we discovered the band of acceptability was three years (between the ages of thirty-nine and forty-two). Older women fade into the woodwork, they explained, but younger women command "the wrong kind" of visibility. Ageism is just another version, it would seem, of the classic catch-22 for professional women: Either they're too feminine (and therefore incompetent) or not feminine enough (and therefore mannish and inauthentic).

The too feminine/not feminine enough double bind, our interviews made clear, turns out to be as paralyzing to ambitious women today as it was to pioneer feminists of the 1970s. Everyone I spoke to expressed relief that those awful days when women donned mannish suits and bow ties are long gone. But everyone also conceded that "getting it right" across all professions and environments was as difficult as ever. Suzi Digby, the British choral conductor, was particularly adamant that women not compromise their femininity. "It's counterproductive, to look like a man," she says. "You give up a card." In her profession, however, this presents special difficulties. Conducting demands she put her back to the audience, a pose that features her posterior. This is an EP challenge for men as well as women, but at least men can wear tails to downplay the distraction: "Women tend to have big bums, and that is bad: It has connotations," she points out. So to downplay the distraction of presenting her backside, and to strike the right silhouette (tall, lean, clean-lined), Digby wears heels and "a well-cut trouser suit." She also ties back her long hair (unless she's on stage with the Rolling Stones, where flying hair is in keeping

with the show). "It's important to get it right," she says. Then she sighs and adds, "I just don't know any women who do."

Getting it wrong has potentially dire consequences, as Carol, a global media firm executive, makes clear. As a twenty-four-year-old analyst at a Swiss investment bank, she was constantly seeking new ways to build client relationships. She struck up a tennis friendship with a male client who was, to her way of thinking "safe"—married, in his fifties, utterly professional in his dealings with her. They played a few Saturdays at his racquet club. On one of these occasions, he showed her some documentation he was looking at to position his firm for a public offering. He wanted Carol's input, and Carol gave it. In exchange, she persuaded him to let her bank handle the offering. "My math and accounting weren't as good as others at the time, but I was young and smart and a good listener," she explains. That IPO turned out to be the biggest piece of business the bank brokered the entire year—an outcome that should have translated into a massive promotion for Carol. But instead her boss threatened to remove her from the account, accusing her of having a sexual affair with the client. His suspicion only grew when the client asked that Carol go to Europe for the road show. "Why do you need to go?" he pressed. "Why does he want you there?"

Carol pointed out the obvious: She'd won the mandate for a global offering, and this was her client. When her boss refused to let her go to Switzerland, the client sent Carol an airline ticket on the Concorde and arranged for her hotel—a gesture that was in keeping with her accomplishment, but that her boss deemed inappropriate. Carol went on the trip but, in light of the rumors, abstained from the after-hours socializing, to the consternation of her client. "I dressed conservatively; I didn't go out at night," she recalls. "I did not want to be perceived as needing to do anything inappropriate to win my deals." But there was no

convincing her boss. "He just couldn't believe I was capable of building a business relationship on the basis of anything other than sex," Carol remarks. Upon her return from the road show, she contacted a headhunter. "There was no way I could stay at that firm. There were too many barriers to my advancement that had nothing to do with my ability," she told me.

From minority women I heard even more harrowing tales about the impossibility of being perceived as professional if you're female (and young, and attractive). Anika, a Pakistani educated in the United States, described a business trip she made to Singapore as a twenty-nine-year-old Big Four accounting consultant. She and her (white male) colleagues were sharing a cab when, to her amazement, they made a detour to a seedy neighborhood where one of them dipped into a doorway and emerged with a prostitute. Stuffed into the cab next to Anika, the prostitute started speaking to her in Malay. "She thought I was a prostitute, too," says Anika. "And I thought, wow. If you're a white guy you're untouchable in this environment, whereas if you're a brown woman with equal or better credentials, you have to work twenty-five times harder to be considered a business professional."

Even when women succeed at telegraphing professionalism, they can still be penalized for being female. Amy, a former bond broker, described her frustration in competing with male brokers whose client-relationship-building toolkit included not just lavish dinners and tickets to cultural events but also late-night visits to strip clubs. "'Let's get you a car and get you home,' the guys would say after we'd all been out to dinner with a bunch of clients," she explained, "because they were 'off to the ballet,' wink-wink, nod-nod." It wasn't fair, she added, because they could bond with the client in a way she couldn't. "To avoid dicey situations, to hold on to my professional reputation," she told us, "I always had to leave early."

## COMMUNICATION

Women seeking to demonstrate leadership by commanding a room run up against an extremely narrow band of acceptability. Over and over we heard male leaders decry the Shrill Woman—a catch-all descriptor for female leaders whose voice, manner, and body language telegraphed inadequate control of their emotions. Crowell & Moring chairman Kent Gardiner described one female associate as so shrill he had to take her off the case. "I think she didn't think she was being listened to," he reflected. "And her reaction was to get very aggressive and pushy without nurturing the client along to where he needed to be . . . on editing briefs, or strategy. The client said, 'I don't want her to run my case anymore.'" Gardiner shook his head, adding, "In this profession, that's like a death sentence." At the same time, however, he said some young women at his firm can speak too tentatively. "It reinforces people's views that you don't know what you're talking about, or that you don't have the courage of your convictions," he tells them. True enough—but where, then, is the sweet spot between too shrill and too tentative?

Many female leaders have yet to find it, our research shows. Recall Margaret Thatcher: She was too shrill, according to her image handlers, yet even after working to modulate her voice she was dogged by harpy imagery, an impression her austere policies fueled. As Bachelet (whom one Chilean described as the "Anti-Thatcher") discovered, there's no getting it right. You're perceived as either hysterical or bloodless; you're seen as either too direct ("ruthless" being a common descriptor) or "too nice," meaning ineffectual. Women who speak confidently about their accomplishments get docked for doing so: 29 percent of our survey respondents identified "tooting your own horn" as a behavior that

detracts from a woman's EP. Yet shrugging off kudos or side-stepping well-earned credit isn't considered very leaderlike either: 24 percent said that "self-deprecating" behavior undermines a woman's EP.

Our qualitative research reveals just how fervently women struggle to be heard without alienating their listeners—and the price they pay for not getting it just right. Anna, a planetary geologist with NASA whom I met when we shared a stage at a conference in Bogotá, Colombia, is a scientist nobody's ever heard of. Yet most of us are familiar with the theory that, 65 million years ago, a gigantic asteroid collided with Earth, an impact that effectively wiped out the dinosaurs and allowed mammals to evolve and dominate. While Anna didn't come up with the theory, she did come up with the evidence that confirmed it: Using state-of-the-art satellite imagery, she found the impact crater. Despite the significance of her discovery, it took her more than a year to get her findings published, and this enormously undermined her efforts to claim credit. Anna is concerned that the delay in publication had a lot to do with a perceived lack of gravitas (her degrees do not come from elite institutions) and communication challenges—she speaks English with a heavy accent. This double whammy makes it difficult for her to be taken seriously by the interplanetary science community. She still struggles to be heard: At a meeting she called recently to pitch her team on the merits of some pricey technology, it was a male colleague who managed, in the end, to win their buy-in. "I'm pretty good at being clear and compelling when I'm presenting an idea in Spanish," she says, reflecting on this experience. "But in English I get too wordy and wishy-washy."

Women who have been more forceful wonder, in turn, if they would have been better off being more restrained. In interviews African-American female executives talked about the need to expose

and disprove the angry black woman stereotypes. "In moments of conflict, you can't afford to reinforce those beliefs," says Rosalind Hudnell, a vice president at Intel. "So what does EP look like, or sound like, in those moments? How do you argue a point without seeming angry or 'not a team player'? If you say 'I don't agree,' or 'I don't want to do that,' as the only black or only woman in the room, you just serve to remind people you're the outlier. There's often no burden on the group to make you feel a part of it; the burden is on you to show you belong. It is unfair but is the reality."

The too blunt/too nice bind, a corollary to the too forceful/too circumspect pitfall, also surfaced in CTI's findings. Our survey data shows that both a "failure to convey empathy" and "being too nice" detract from a woman's EP. Just as many (15 percent) believe that "being too nice" and "not being nice enough" detract from a woman's EP. A number of women we interviewed spoke of their frustration in trying to find the space in between. Debbie Maples, a loss-prevention vice president at the Gap, described a typical circumstance: By nature a "very direct, very strong" communicator, she was told by a coach early in her career that "honey attracts more bees than vinegar," so she took pains to rein in her candor and soften her opinions. A few years later when she started at the Gap, she says, her boss told her she was way too nice. "Where's the balance?" she muses. "Do they want me to be harder or softer? With men or with women? With my superiors or my subordinates? It's tricky to figure out."

## GRAVITAS

The trickiest EP terrain a woman must navigate concerns her gravitas, where the forceful-but-unlikable chasm yawns the widest. A woman who shows teeth, for example—who is decisive,

assertive, and willing to hold her ground—risks being perceived as a bitch, or noncooperative ("not a team player"). Linda, a global corporate services executive at a multinational corporation, bumped up against this bind early in her career: If she came on strong in an effort to make a point, her (male) superiors viewed her as argumentative and not open to others' input. "They told me I wasn't a change agent, I was too much a naysayer," she recalls, "when I was just trying to get them to see another point of view!" She toughed it out, and today, she says, her gravitas as a leader specifically derives from her extreme candor. "People come to me because they don't want the sugarcoated message that's out there," she explains. "Nine times out of ten, they will say, 'I came to you because I want to hear what is really going on.'" Looking back she still bristles at having been singled out for a criticism that would not have been levied on her male colleagues for exhibiting the same behaviors. "A man is viewed as a strong personality if he is arguing a point, whereas a woman arguing the same point is viewed as a bitch and heartily disliked," she observes.

Michelle Obama learned this, as most women do, the hard way. On the campaign trail in early 2008, taking the national stage for the first time, she spoke her mind: She told her audience how she really felt as a black woman witnessing the nation's revitalized interest in the political process. "For the first time in my adult lifetime, I am really proud of my country," she said. Within hours, the press branded her an Angry Black Woman. The conservative press gleefully took her to task for her lukewarm patriotism, flushing an apology from candidate Obama, who claimed his wife didn't mean what she said. Headlines in both the *New York Times* and the *Los Angeles Times* pegged her as "a potential liability" for the Democratic nominee;[95] one Fox News commentator went so far as to label the fist-bump she shared with her victorious husband "a terrorist fist jab."[96] The militant image dogged her in the early days

of her husband's first term, so she dug into good works benefiting military families and launching her Get Moving campaign to tackle childhood obesity—causes chosen in part because they were so very safe. First ladies, she was made to realize, are not allowed to take on anything remotely controversial.

Bottom line? Behaviors that confer gravitas on a man by demonstrating he can "show teeth"—offering candid assessments, interjecting opinions, hammering home a point, banging a fist, showing anger, dropping the F-bomb—come off as aggression in a woman. Consider the flap that erupted in June 2013 when Paula Deen, celebrity chef and the self-described Queen of Butter, admitted to using the N-word. Ballantine canceled her five-book deal, companies yanked away their endorsement contracts, and Deen was left twisting in the wind. Yet when Alec Baldwin, the *30 Rock* star, tweeted to a British reporter some gay-bashing threats ("I'm gonna find you, George Stark, you toxic little queen, and I'm gonna fuck . . . you . . . up," followed by, "I'd put my foot up your fucking ass, George Stark, but I'm sure you'd dig it too much"), the backlash was virtually nonexistent.[97] Baldwin apologized, as he has done in the past, for his hotheadedness (this is a man who left a voice mail with his eleven-year-old daughter calling her a "thoughtless little pig").[98] The incidents and his response have, if anything, burnished his image as an alpha male.

Making this worse, of course, is that men don't see the double standard even as they apply it. In our focus groups male managers delighted in inventorying for us female leaders whom the public had vilified for abrasiveness (Yahoo's Marissa Mayer as well as HP's former CEO Carly Fiorina). But these same managers detected no irony in likewise complaining about female subordinates who embarrassed them in important meetings by being overly deferential or not making their points forcefully enough. Our survey results captured it perfectly: 31 percent of our respondents said that being

"too bossy" undermines a woman's EP, and 31 percent said being "too passive" undermines a woman's EP. Go figure.

Speaking truth to power and showing teeth aren't the only gravitas-building behaviors that women can't get right. Reputation, too, turns out to be a double-edged sword for women. Consider that of Christine Lagarde, head of the IMF. Lagarde's credentials, track record, and experience are impeccable, as even her detractors concede. "Altogether, she conforms to a profile common to women who project a steady hand and a cool head and are therefore acceptable to men as leaders of male-dominated organizations," observed Diane Johnson in *Vogue* in September 2011, noting that "Lagarde is five foot ten, handsome, poised, perfect, exuding confidence and charm, like a glamorous headmistress her students half fall in love with, half fear."[99] Yet for these charms, Lagarde is likewise held in contempt. When she took the reins of the IMF from the scandal-plagued Dominique Strauss-Kahn in July 2011, she was criticized for being "an upper-class woman cut off from common people and more preoccupied with her look than their welfare, the way such elegant, chic people are."[100] In other words, because she positively radiated executive presence, Lagarde wasn't *populist* enough as a person.

Debbie Storey, who heads up talent development for AT&T, notes a difference in people's reaction to books on leadership authored by men and women—in part because women authors tend to include stories about how they've had to balance their roles as caregivers with their careers as they climbed the corporate ladder. "When powerful men write books about leadership, they tend to leave out the support systems that played a big role in making their success possible," she explained. "You don't read about the stay-at-home spouse who enabled them to more easily achieve balance.

"Women authors, on the other hand, usually tackle these issues head-on, which makes them vulnerable and frequently trig-

gers judgment. Too often, they're judged against themselves—and held to a different standard. They're often viewed as not credible unless they're near-perfect. So in addition to being an accomplished leader, they also have to be role-model mothers, wives, friends, volunteers, et cetera."

## HOW TO WIN GREATER LATITUDE: INSIGHTS AND STRATEGIES

### WHEN YOU SHOW TEETH, SHOW THAT YOU HAVE THE BEST INTERESTS OF THE TEAM AT HEART

Assert your difference of opinion, but take the "I" out of your argument, advises Intel's Rosalind Hudnell, a leader who's perfected the art of "arguing with grace." Too often, she says, women and people of color set themselves up to be branded "not a team player" by framing their argument in terms of what's bugging them personally. "Don't make it about yourself, because that only underscores your status as the outsider," says Hudnell. "Remember, when you're working for a company, you're responsible to that company. Whatever you're going to argue, whatever decision you don't like or want to push back on, you need to come not from a position of what's good for you but of what's best for the company. Be deliberate with your language. Be careful about your tone and your body language. Consider the perspective of the majority. You'll be far more effective if before taking a stand you consider, 'How will this idea be heard by those in power?'"

### WHEN SPEAKING TRUTH TO POWER, WIDEN YOUR BAND OF RECEPTIVITY WITH A JUDICIOUS USE OF HUMOR

Stella, a global leader on our task force, tells of a boss she had whom she admired tremendously for his intelligence, his knowl-

edge of the business, and his ability to analyze a situation and render a decision. She did not, however, admire his leadership style, which was so abrasive that he effectively preempted any and all pushback. "He'd pound the table, curse, and denigrate anyone who took issue with his analysis," she says, "and it worked: He was so intimidating no one dared to challenge him." But Stella isn't a person who keeps her thoughts to herself when she knows she's right, so when her boss gathered his team to discuss implementing a new sales strategy, one that he believed would drive revenue, Stella refused to be intimidated. "I believed his approach would have a negative impact on customer satisfaction, and therefore on revenue," she recalls, "so I countered his position, not confrontationally, but objectively." He went nuclear. "Goddammit!" he shouted, striking the table with his fist and glaring at everyone around the table. "Does anyone want a piece of Stella before I get mine?" For two heartbeats, Stella remembers, the room went absolutely silent. Then she said, "No, Bob, they're waiting to see you do it." Bob burst out laughing.

Stella did another thing to ensure her remarks enhanced rather than detracted from her gravitas: After the meeting concluded, she sought out her boss to explain that she hadn't been contradicting him but rather ensuring he had the knowledge he needed to render the right decision. "I just want to make sure you had the whole picture," she told him. "If you go in a different direction, okay, but it's my responsibility to put the facts on the table so that every one of your decisions is fully informed." He told her he appreciated her intent, and admired her for her courage. "His respect for me probably tripled as a result of that encounter," Stella says.

HIT THE MARK BY TAKING MORE CAREFUL AIM

Too often, says AllianceBernstein's Lori Massad, women take a broad-spectrum approach to communication that leaves them

open to crossfire. Instead of listening to others' views, they blurt out their own first; instead of sharing their best insight, they download everything that's occurred to them; and instead of waiting for an opening that might maximize receptivity, they stream consciousness. Better to be a sniper, says Massad: Pick your target, pick your moment, and fire your best shot. "If I am participating in a meeting, my first communication cannot be meek," she explains. "I do not speak up unless I have a really good point to make or insight to add. I usually wait to speak until I am prepared to make a counterpoint, or ask an insightful question." The opposite applies, she stresses, if she's leading the meeting. "I take charge immediately by offering a bold statement. I do not do small talk or ask about people's weekends or their family. 'Here is what I need. Here is my objective. Let's get started.'"

## BUILD A PERSONAL BRAND THAT GRANTS YOU LOTS OF LATITUDE TO BE YOU—AND BE RELENTLESS IN PROJECTING IT

Take a page out of Richard Branson's playbook. The CEO of all things Virgin cast himself early on as an iconoclast, someone who delighted in taking on challenges and doing things differently. That brand has inoculated him from criticism on a number of fronts; indeed, Branson generates as much revenue from his failures as he does from his successes because his brand—embracing challenge, doing things differently—celebrates the attempt, not the outcome. Consider the bet he made with rival airline owner Tony Fernandes: Depending on whose Formula One racing team finished lower in the standings, the loser had to serve as a cabin steward on the other's airline. Branson lost the bet but reinvigorated his brand by dressing up as a stewardess and putting in a full shift on AirAsia. The stunt endeared him to his public (and apparently to passenger Desmond Tutu, who told him he was "vo-

luptuous"), boosted both airlines' revenues, and raised three hundred thousand dollars for the Starlight Children's Foundation.[101] I'm not saying you need go to such extremes, of course. But a consciously built and confidently maintained brand that positions you outside the box goes a long way in ensuring that others won't dare box you in.

## BUY MORE EP LATITUDE BY WIELDING YOUR CREDENTIALS MORE CONSCIOUSLY

CTI's director of research, Laura Sherbin, wields some impressive credentials, including a Ph.D. in economics. But back when she joined our organization in 2007, she struggled to exude gravitas because she looked young—young enough to be thought of as a student of mine at Columbia, rather than someone credentialed enough and experienced enough to teach her own course (she is currently an adjunct professor at Columbia's School of International and Public Affairs). How did she handle this? Whenever it made sense, she (tactfully) requested to be introduced as Dr. Laura Sherbin, and when presenting our research to an external or new audience, she worked in mention of her faculty position at Columbia.

## SHOW YOU CARE

For women in particular, winning more latitude in the public's eye depends on showcasing activities that demonstrate you care about the disenfranchised. This works wonders on the likability front. Indeed, you won't find a female leader out there who *hasn't* come to embrace this tactic. Kirsten Gillibrand, Hillary Clinton's replacement as the junior Senator from New York State, has become a voice against sexual assaults in the military;[102] Elizabeth Warren, in her run-up to winning a Massachusetts U.S. senatorial seat, recorded a contribution for the "It Gets Better" video

campaign to help bullied LGBT teenagers.[103] Both women have learned, it would seem, from Hillary's mistakes.

Feedback can be helpful in pointing out which paths to take—and which pitfalls to avoid—but at a certain point, many people feel constrained by parameters that narrow the choices between comfort and conformity. Yet walking that fine line is the ultimate test of executive presence.

# AUTHENTICITY VS. CONFORMITY

Last June in London I met with Trevor Phillips, the former chair of the Equality and Human Rights Commission (EHRC), over breakfast at the Covent Garden Hotel.

"The most extraordinary thing just happened," he said, sinking into the purple upholstery across from me. He then proceeded to tell me how, a block from the hotel, he'd been approached on the street by a total stranger, a man who'd recognized him as the former host of *The London Programme* but also as the producer of *Windrush*, the 1998 BBC television series documenting the rise of multiracial Britain.

"He wanted me to know that, as a young black Brit, *Windrush* had changed his life," Phillips continued. "He'd gotten the DVDs and shared them with his children, because he knew they'd come away just as inspired." Phillips shook his head, marveling at the encounter. "Making that series was probably the riskiest move I ever made, but also the most important and the one for which I'll be ever grateful. It returned me to myself."

Outspoken about LGBT rights, a vehement defender of free speech, yet vocal in his opposition to multiculturalism, Phillips had just stepped down from the top slot at the EHRC, which he'd formed in 2006 from the ashes of the Commission for Racial Equality, which he had also chaired. I remember being utterly wowed by his sheer presence. A tall, impeccably dressed,

extremely well-spoken Afro-Caribbean man blessed with both an Imperial College British accent and a broadcaster's deep voice, Phillips emanates authority and credibility, and talks eloquently and easily about the complexity of multiracial Britain. Knowing something of his political career—he'd been friends with Tony Blair, a London mayoral candidate in 1999, and chair of the London Assembly until 2003—I assumed that he'd forged that career around his multicultural identity.

But in fact, not until he was thirty-eight years old did Phillips come to embrace, as he puts it, his "first language." Born in London to parents who'd emigrated from Guyana, Phillips readily adapted to British ways of speaking, dressing, and socializing, becoming so fluent in this "second language" that, after graduating with a chemistry degree from Imperial College London, he had few qualms about forsaking his origins. Embarking on a career in television, he quickly rose in the ranks, becoming head of current affairs for London Weekend Television (LWT) in 1994. To have gotten so far by his late thirties was an extraordinary achievement. He seemed poised for a top leadership role. Instead, he turned away.

"As you climb the ladder as a black professional, you get to a place where you're confronted with a choice," he explained to me. "You can either resurrect that first language, give it weight and heft in your new high-profile life—a risky business—or you can play it safe, and continue to speak your second language so that you can survive and thrive in a white world.

"I'd reached that fork in the road," he continued, "because I was burning to make this documentary on *Windrush*, the troops ship that brought the first West Indian immigrants to Britain in 1948. And I knew ITV [then LWT] wasn't about to sign on. They didn't see it as an important project. I'd have to leave to produce it, and I knew once I stepped off track there was no coming back."

But step off he did, forming his own production company. He then went on to create a partnership with the BBC, producing his documentary as a four-part television series. When it garnered rave reviews, he teamed up with his brother Michael, a novelist born in Guyana, to write the underlying story, which Harper-Collins published to great critical acclaim.

"*Windrush* was a huge success," he reflected. "And transformative for me. Firstly, it gave me enormous satisfaction. But it also made me into a public figure and put me on the map in ways I couldn't possibly have anticipated. It was a turning point, no question about it. Because by embracing what was most meaningful to me," Phillips added, "I forged a career path where that suppressed identity could flourish."

## BLEACHED-OUT PROFESSIONALS

In late 2011 and early 2012, when CTI first probed the topic of executive presence with focus groups at Moody's, the Gap, EY, and Freddie Mac, we uncovered a potent source of anguish for up-and-coming professionals of color. While EP for some was a set of unwritten rules that no one had bothered to share with them, for others it was a terrain they felt they couldn't navigate without sacrificing core aspects of their identity. To use the metaphor that Trevor Phillips shared with me, they were all "bilingual," high-performing managers who grew up with a distinct heritage and a "first language" but learned to survive and thrive in a white world by adopting the conventions of that world—in effect a second language. Indeed, they had the track record, credentials, and experience to get to the next level, and understood they were being scrutinized for their EP. But they were also, to invoke an older metaphor, "bleached-out professionals," individuals who in

order to be perceived as professionals in their work environments had effectively scrubbed themselves of all ethnic, religious, racial, socioeconomic, and educational identifiers.[104] And they weren't happy about it. Like Phillips, they had reached that place on the ladder where looking and acting like a leader at work suddenly didn't seem to be worth the sacrifice of their "other" identity, of their first language. They resented the pressure to conform. They couldn't justify bleaching out aspects of themselves in order to fit in. In short, they were at a crossroads: Would they plow forward by suppressing their difference—or by asserting it? By fitting in—or standing out? By conforming to the culture in which they found themselves—or owning their authenticity?

The results of our national survey in 2012 brought this conflict into sharper focus. Forty-one percent of professionals of color said they had felt the need to compromise their authenticity in order to conform to EP standards at their company. White respondents also conceded they felt the need to conform, of course, but people of color were significantly more likely than whites to feel this tension. Among people of color, respondents of Asian descent were afflicted the most—particularly Asian men. Among women of color, Hispanics were the likeliest to say they'd sacrificed authenticity in order to conform. Across the board, a majority of professionals of color (56 percent) told us they felt held to a stricter code of EP than their Caucasian peers. Overwhelmingly, the EP code they feel impelled to fit into is that embodied by white men.

This should come as no surprise. Everywhere you look—on magazine covers, websites, online journals, industry reports—you will find that corporate leaders in America are nearly always depicted as white men. A quick sampling of the magazines in our office archive reveals just how easy it is to conflate "the right stuff" of leadership with a certain phenotype. Above headlines such as "The Tests of a Leader" (*Harvard Business Review*, Janu-

ary 2007) or "The Four Types of CEOs" (*Strategy + Business*, May 2011) you'll find someone who looks like Mitt Romney.

What does conforming to this standard entail? For people of color, it means expending energy to repress ethnic identifiers in appearance, speech, behavior, and background. In our survey, a majority of Asian, African-American, and Hispanic respondents agreed with the statement "I have deliberately changed the way I tell my personal story in order to bolster my professional image." Alarmingly, the more senior the respondent, the more likely he or she was to agree with the statement. This choice might reflect the realities confronted by an older generation. Then again, it might mean that the pathway to the top imposes increasingly heavy sacrifices for professionals of color.

*Invisible Lives*, a report CTI published in late 2005, was among the first to document the nature and extent of this sacrifice.[105] Coauthored by myself and Cornel West, the report quantifies not only the terrible cost to minority professionals who feel obliged to cordon off their church, community, and family lives in order to succeed at work, but also the cost to their employers, who miss out on the leadership skills minority professionals develop outside of work because they leave much of who they are at home. Stephanie, an African-American manager we interviewed who worked for a major fashion brand, illustrates perfectly the lose-lose of bleached-out professionalism. Stephanie had poured her heart into a weekend tutoring program she ran at a homeless shelter in Newark, New Jersey, a commitment that meant she had to leave her Manhattan office on occasion at 4:30 p.m. on Friday. Even though she arrived at 7 a.m. on that day, she was acutely aware that, to her boss, her early departure signaled a lack of commitment. Yet she would not speak to him about her community involvement because she was fearful that if he knew he would see her through a new lens—not as an accomplished professional but

as a black girl from the ghetto. So Stephanie kept quiet about her volunteer role, despite the fact that her work with homeless children won her a Future Leader Today award in a ceremony at the White House. Her lack of candor wasn't good for her or the company. She was passed over for a promotion (her boss continued to see her as disengaged). Shortly thereafter she left the company.

Like so many other minority professionals we interviewed, Stephanie saw herself as two people operating in two irreconcilable spheres: the highly effective and committed leader in her community, and the bleached-out professional on the job. To reveal one aspect of her identity in the other sphere would be to provide her employer with "ammunition," or evidence that could be used against her to the degree that it reinforces racial stereotypes—a distrust that more than half of minority women we surveyed own up to feeling.[106]

Our EP focus groups and interviews reaffirmed these findings from our 2005 study: Non-Caucasians expend an awful lot of energy cordoning off aspects of their personal lives. They don't share, because they don't feel comfortable sharing, what they're most impassioned about, lest details about their children or political leanings or community involvement undermine the impression they're like everybody else at the firm. "For a long time I have left a large part of 'me' at home—the 'me' who has strong opinions on cultural and political issues—and adopted a persona at work that is more conservative, less forthcoming, than I would otherwise be," an Asian-American financial analyst explained. "The problem is the longer you do that, the more alienated you become because you are shutting off whole parts of yourself—and the more of yourself you risk losing."

Walling off parts of your life will cost you not just personally but also professionally. Ray, an accountant, was for years two people: the person at work who conformed to the way everybody

else looked and acted and sounded, and the person outside work who had southern roots, a southern drawl, and strong ties to his church and African-American community. Recently he's taken steps to reconcile those two personas, having taken a lead role in his firm's black affinity group. But his decision to no longer "hide" is due more to resignation, he says, than a change in the cultural climate at work. "I've gotten to the point where I no longer care," Ray explains. "I'm not going to rise up the ladder at this company; I can't even get on the teams or the projects where I could contribute valuable skills, even though I have twice the experience of some of my colleagues. It's a case of the invisible man: the less you get to be yourself, the less likely others are to remember you for high-visibility assignments and less visible you will indeed become."

The experience of minority professionals parallels that of another group: LGBT professionals who feel obliged to pass for straight at work. Nearly half of the gay professionals we surveyed for our 2011 report, *The Power of "Out": LGBT in the Workplace*, said they remained closeted at work for fear of being ostracized by their colleagues and penalized professionally by their superiors.[107] One-third of them literally live double lives, out to friends and family, but not to their coworkers and superiors. Whether partially or fully closeted, however, these individuals expend considerable energy on remaining "off the gaydar" of their colleagues on the job, watching their pronouns, lying about their significant others, or just not volunteering personal information at the water cooler or lunch table. And as with minority professionals, that expenditure costs them both personally and professionally. More than half of closeted LGBT workers told us they feel stalled in their careers, compared with the 36 percent of gay employees who are out at work. They're more disengaged, too: They were 73 percent more likely than their out counterparts to say they intended

to leave their firm within three years. But even as being in the closet corrodes their productivity, fear of being found out keeps them there. They become masters of neutrality and control—an iteration on the bleached-out professional syndrome that minorities describe.

African-Americans in particular spoke to us of their struggle to conform to EP standards at work in terms of their communication. They're careful to modulate their voice, tone, and language lest they affirm "historically embedded notions of being aggressive, angry people, people who will blow up," as one interviewee put it. Joel Tealer, senior vice president of human resources, Strategic Business Units at Chubb Insurance Groups, says he's learned to be "very careful" about the language he uses in any emotionally charged or fraught discussion. "As a multicultural manager, I need to be sure I'm balanced, because if I'm not—if I'm loud or animated or left-of-center—my audience, if they're outside my culture, will judge me as less professional. White males have the ability to be further to the left and a little more animated when discussing volatile topics without being viewed negatively."

African-American women likewise told us how carefully they step in order to tamp down the specter of the angry black woman, behavior that exacts a toll not only on their authenticity, points out Judith Harrison, chief diversity officer at Weber Shandwick, but also on their productivity. "That struggle to muzzle themselves is just a sinkhole in terms of the time and energy it requires," she says. "And that time could be so much better spent."

Given these significant costs, why do professionals of color take such pains to rein in or paper over who they are to accommodate the expectations of their Caucasian peers and superiors? Because when you trumpet your difference, or make no effort to mute it, you are even more likely to become a target of unconscious bias or even overt discrimination.

For minorities as well as gays, the corporate landscape bristles with land mines in the form of slights or snubs that serve as reminders of latent discrimination. Terri Austin, an attorney and chief diversity officer at McGraw-Hill Financial who previously served as chief compliance officer at AIG, recalls a C-suite meeting of the company during which the leading officer turned to her, the only woman and the only African-American in the room, to request that she take the minutes. "He was serious!" she says, still incredulous that, among equals at that table, she would be called out to render a secretary's services. Fortunately her sponsor, who was then general counsel, intervened to insist that someone else be brought in to perform the task, as Austin wasn't to do it. But the incident underscored for her the difficulties faced by executives of color operating in the uppermost tiers of management.

That racism still presses a heavy thumb on qualified minority professionals is affirmed by the results of our EP survey. Hispanics, we found, are nearly three times more likely than their white colleagues to be mistaken for someone's secretary or assistant. Twenty-two percent of African-Americans say they're frequently mistaken for someone else of their own race. Most distressingly, fully 19 percent of African-Americans say their colleagues perceive them as "affirmative-action hires." Across the board, minorities remain highly skeptical of their chances of success. More than a third of African-American respondents believe that a person of color would never get a top job at their company, a perception echoed by almost as many Asians and Hispanics.

So while the United States has made significant progress in providing equal access to higher education, and equal access to white-collar jobs, progression to the upper echelons of management is still extremely problematic for people of color. Confronted with Trevor Phillips's fork in the road, most opt to continue hiding their difference lest it limit their ascent. Phillips's protégé

David, a Brit of Afro-Caribbean heritage, is a case in point: Recently offered the position of chair of the black executive network at his company, he turned it down, explaining to Phillips that becoming "a poster child" for black employees was just too risky. "He sees the whole D&I [diversity and inclusiveness] mandate as a burden," Phillips clarified for me. "He feels it will get in the way of him being taken seriously as a professional at the firm."

## RESOLVING THE TENSION

So to return to our question: If you're different from most people at work, do you suppress that difference or embrace it in order to be perceived as leadership material?

Everyone we surveyed or spoke to affirmed the importance of authenticity, pointing out that no leader can win or retain followers without it. Everyone also agreed that succeeding in any organizational culture demands that you make accommodations to that culture. Even straight white men will be obliged to conform, whether by dressing more formally than they'd like or reining in their happy-hour jokes or purging their Facebook walls of incriminating photos. And conformity is hardly a corporate phenomenon: Small businesses ask that their employees mold themselves to fit the path carved by the owner; educators operate within the boundaries established by their school boards, which are informed by state laws; public-sector employees answer to officials who answer to the public. For-profit or nonprofit, ultimately every organization operates within a narrow band of customer or shareholder or board approval. Even rule breakers like Groupon's Andrew Mason, who seemingly reinvent the marketplace, must answer to the strictures imposed by that new marketplace—or be shoved aside and forced to reinvent themselves again. No matter

who we are and where we work, that is, the workplace imposes norms around appearance, communication, and gravitas that we'd be fools to ignore if our intent is to thrive and not just survive.

Hence it may be helpful to discern where assimilating is tantamount to "playing the game" as opposed to "selling out." Lawrence, an insurance industry senior vice president, notes that conforming doesn't necessarily involve a cost, and may even confer a benefit. By way of example, he describes his reasons for taking up golf, a sport that certainly wasn't prevalent in the African-American community where he grew up. But, recognizing its power as a conversation piece, he applied himself to the sport—and discovered he absolutely loved it. "Did it compromise me, to assimilate in this way? I don't think so," he reflects. "Ultimately succeeding is about networking and engaging with people. If you're trying to get to know someone, an executive or senior leader, someone you don't know much about or have much in common, you need to focus on what they do and where their interests lie. And if there's an opportunity to get involved in something that creates common ground, then you'd best take it, because it will give you the venue to share your personality." Reflecting on his rapid ascent within the firm, Lawrence adds, "In assimilating, you may find that you're changing yourself more than they're changing you—and in very positive ways."

Michael, another insurance executive, observes that accusing you of selling out can be your peer group's way of ensuring you don't break from their ranks. A small number of African-American colleagues who were great friends with him at the dawn of their careers together later rebuked him, Michael recalls, when he started differentiating himself in terms of seizing stretch opportunities and establishing strategic relationships. "Oh, you're kissing up? You've decided you're going to be white?" they taunted. Michael shrugged it off. "I've had people ever since I started to rise in management

accuse me of not being true to myself or my heritage because I was doing what the successful majority of people in the organization do to get ahead," he explains. "Well, what's selling out? Working extra hours? Volunteering for assignments? Taking on more responsibility? That's doing your job, *plus*—and that is going to get you ahead. I've found that sometimes when a group starts questioning your authenticity, then that's the group trying to hold you back."

The difficulty, of course, is that only *you* can determine what constitutes a compromise to your authenticity, as opposed to just a compromise. To help you make that call, I've amassed strategic and tactical advice from professionals of color who've been down this same road.

## TACTICS

### KNOW YOUR "NON-NEGOTIABLES" AND WALK AWAY

Some cultures simply don't deserve your compliance. Weber Shandwick's Judith Harrison recalls how early in her career she worked in an Arthur Young office where the office manager, who was also the head of HR, displayed an enormous Confederate flag over her desk. Harrison, who is African-American, labored for several years in this environment until she realized that the stress of working for a leader whom she couldn't respect and who couldn't perceive her value was taking a toll on her health. "I had to remove myself," she says. "It was making me physically sick, going into that situation every day, knowing that people did not see me the way I knew I deserved to be seen. Nothing is worth that."

In hindsight, however, she's glad to have had such a test at the outset of her career. "I think that it enabled me to develop strength in my convictions about what was important and what wasn't, and to maintain confidence in myself."

## Authenticity vs. Conformity

### NEVER TRY TO BE SOMEONE YOU'RE NOT

Barbara Adachi, the first woman at Deloitte ever to head up a region, didn't set out to be a trailblazer. Indeed, her tactic upon being hired decades ago was to simply emulate the "very strong" woman who was her first boss, as there were precious few other women to look up to as role models. Adachi, a petite woman of Japanese descent, was surprised at her boss's client approach and style—she was very aggressive and often swore, but nonetheless was very effective with clients. Thinking this might be the path to success, Adachi convinced herself to adopt it on her next prospective client cold call.

She bombed.

"Oh, it was awful," Adachi exclaims. "'*Who do you think you are, talking to me like that,*'" the client on the other end of the phone had asked her, incredulous. "'*You're not my wife!*'" It was a searing lesson for her in the importance of developing executive presence within her own style boundaries. "My boss could get away with it, but it just wasn't me," she reflects. "I was never going to be the loudest voice in the room, though I was under pressure to try. I had to accept that wasn't my style and it could never work for me."

Her own style has served her well: a board member and partner, this last year she retired from Deloitte as national managing director for U.S. Human Capital (HC) Consulting.

### PLAY THE LONG GAME

Carolyn Buck Luce, a partner at EY for more than twenty years, makes clear the imperative of taking the long view on your career when confronted with challenges that demand you sacrifice some aspect of your true self. Ten years into her career at EY, after building a number of boutique businesses for the firm in the national strategy group, Carolyn recognized that she was "confusing

my job description with the job I was paid to do." She realized, she explains, that to fulfill her life mission as a change agent she needed to change how she operated within the firm. "To play a maverick role in a traditional company was a recipe for disaster," she says. "I was really feeling the pressure of being misunderstood: It was getting harder to win support. If I wanted to use this firm as a platform for my larger mission as a champion of women in the workplace, I would be better off taking a traditional job that everyone could understand—and then do it in an untraditional way."

So she left the strategy group to take up fieldwork as an account manager, a move that quickly granted her the opportunity to grow EY's expertise in the health-care sector. Over the next ten years, she built a billion-dollar business in the global life sciences space—the job she was paid to do—while at the same time building women's networks, shoring up the firm's commitment to diversity and inclusion, and growing the Task Force for Talent Innovation with a group of like-minded corporate leaders. All of these roles comprised her job *description*, as she sees it.

"You've got to have the vision and write the path," she adds. "It's your responsibility to figure out how to align your talents and gifts to the culture so that, long-term, you achieve your goals. When you are the curator of your authenticity, you can invest intentionally—and then it's a win-win for you *and* your company."

## PERCEIVE SLIGHTS AS OPPORTUNITIES TO ADDRESS IGNORANCE

Michael, the senior executive we met earlier, describes how, when he moved to San Jose, California, with his company, the branch manager would arrive each week and, moving from one end of the hall to the other, dip in to each leader's office to say hello and chitchat about the weekend, the kids, and interesting new

projects in play. "Then he'd come to my office," relates Michael. "'Hey, Michael, what's going on?' he'd ask—and he'd move right on to the next person." As the only minority in the company's leadership it was easy, says Michael, to conclude that he was being slighted. And it occurred to him to respond like someone who'd been slighted. "I remember thinking, 'If he's not going to get to know me, then I am going to some other company,'" Michael explains.

But he quickly realized he'd likely suffer from a career standpoint if he ignored the situation instead of addressing it head-on. So he took the initiative, seeking out the branch manager at every opportunity. "If he came in early, I came in early and found him," says Michael. "I talked to him about things and found out what he was involved in and interested in. We talked about our families. It got to the point where I couldn't get him out of my office and get work done."

He adds, "It's so easy to think that every slight might have something to do with your background or gender. It's not to say there are no real snubs, but I've found that more often than not somebody's coming from a place of ignorance rather than bigotry. If you're overly sensitive to the possibility of intentional slights and withdraw as a result, you freeze yourself rather than move forward."

## SEEK AIR COVER BEFORE YOU STEP OUT TO ASSERT YOUR AUTHENTICITY

One of the high points of her career, says Helen, a former director at a Silicon Valley firm, was being praised for her executive presence by the firm's CEO—in front of 1,200 of the firm's top leaders. "Yesterday was an outstanding day for the women of this firm," said the CEO as he opened the annual directors-and-above meeting, "and I want to personally thank Helen for her standout leadership."

He then asked her to stand up and be applauded by the mostly male audience. "I never felt so proud," says Helen, shaking her head in disbelief. "I think sometimes, as women and as minorities, we avoid the spotlight because we're afraid we're going to pay a penalty for standing out and earning the admiration and praise of executives. But we can't let that fear stop us. We simply have to embrace who we are and learn to take credit for our successes."

She didn't get to bask in the glow of that success for long, however. Her sudden visibility threatened her then boss, she says, who went out of his way to keep her offstage and out of the CEO's view. "The more presence I developed—I had the CEO's executive coach working with me—the more brutally critical of me he became," says Helen, a Latina with a master's degree in industrial engineering as well as a master's from Stanford in executive education. "'Why are you talking to him?' he'd question me. 'You stay here, I'll go deliver the numbers.'" As a result of the browbeating, she felt her confidence and control dissipate. "I didn't know how to fight, so I did what I shouldn't have: I let my emotions show when he would interrupt me during a presentation. I had no grace under fire."

She might have weathered the assaults had her ally, the head of HR, not left the firm. But in the wake of her departure, Helen says, she was completely sponsorless. "I didn't have a well-placed senior person to help me navigate," she says, "someone looking out for me, someone who would run interference with my boss or secure me the CEO's protection. You've got to have that air cover so that when you finally take the stage, everyone knows not to challenge your claim to it." A few months later a demoralized and dispirited Helen left the company.

## LEVERAGE YOUR BACKGROUND

Ripa Rashid, currently director of research and curriculum for the Iclif Leadership and Governance Centre in Kuala Lumpur, Ma-

laysia, was born in Bangladesh and grew up in Australia, Bangladesh, and Malaysia before coming to the United States to earn her bachelor's in astrophysics from Harvard. But Rashid didn't perceive the value of her global upbringing until ten years into her career as a management consultant, when a vacancy in the diversity office opened up at her firm. She took the job and, in managing a team that focused on retaining and developing women as leaders, built a stunningly successful mentoring initiative that launched in Europe and won traction abroad precisely because she had the cultural smarts to make it relevant outside the United States. "All the many pieces of my identity—being South Asian, living in many countries, training as a management consultant—went into my effectiveness," Rashid observes. "And because I brought this multifaceted and international background, these programs had a global lens. They didn't suffer from that U.S.-centric stigma."

At every job thereafter, Rashid capitalized on her multicultural background, capturing insights that colleagues who didn't have those stripes of having lived and worked all over the world might well have missed. When she and I were working on our book on emerging markets, for example, one interviewee confided in her, "I don't want to hear that emerging-market women are desperately behind those in the West"—an observation that shaped our thesis and one that likely this interviewee wouldn't have shared with me, a non-Muslim, Welsh-born woman.[108]

Today, living and working across Asia, Rashid feels she's come full circle in finding, refining, and leveraging her personal brand. "I'm like a chameleon," she laughs. "I've walked in so many shoes, I see the world through multiple lenses. When I'm in India, people assume I was born there; when I'm in Europe, people know I've worked and lived there. People open up to me. In research, nothing is more important than getting candid answers."

DIFFERENTIATE YOURSELF BY WHAT MAKES YOU DIFFERENT

Linda, the retail product executive we met earlier, learned early in her career that her roots—she grew up in Africa—were going to assert themselves. "I hardly ever sound like anyone else in the room," she says. "People try to piece together where I'm from, because I've spent a lot of time in London, but it's mostly Africa that comes through, and it's just different from anything they've ever heard."

It took her a while to realize, however, that her accent would get her heard in ways her female colleagues could not. "Women are more likely to be screened out and not heard than men," she observes. "I am less likely, because I sound different and look different. I decided this was an opportunity to stand out and be differentiated versus something to worry about."

In the end it is these powerful inescapable differences that most distinguish her as a leader. "I have an advantage as a black woman from Africa," she elaborates, "because by definition, at my table, we are not all alike. We will have to be more tolerant and open. It's an advantage that a white male executive may not have: Everyone must be much more intentional about how they express themselves. No one on my team would ever come to me with the statement, 'So-and-so may not be capable because she's a woman.' It is pretty clear that that sort of thing will not fly. The leaders on my team, their perceptions of women and black people are shaped by spending time with me. So then, that trickles down to their team."

In 2012, a diversity magazine named Linda as one of their top executive leaders under age fifty, honoring her for bringing her distinctive brand and values to the teams she manages worldwide. "People are afraid to talk about gender and race," she says. "I'm better able than most to create an environment where it's possible to have an open, honest dialogue—and not hide behind some of the politically correct labels—to get at what the real issues are."

## UNDERSTAND THE DIVERSITY DIVIDEND

In figuring out the hows and whys of lifting up your authenticity in the workplace, consider how the landscape for multicultural professionals is shifting. As our economy grows ever more globalized, and competition for market share intensifies, companies are under ever greater pressure to innovate—both to retain market share and capture new markets in emerging economies and underserved markets. New research we've conducted at CTI reveals that, by representing some of those underleveraged markets, female and multicultural employees hold the key to innovating more effectively for them.[109] In other words, your inherent difference makes you a valuable asset to teams—and leaders—who might benefit from the unique perspective that difference confers. Your understanding of clients and consumers outside your colleagues' experience can help them better identify—and address—the needs of those clients and consumers.

Other CTI research shows that innate diversity on teams—having members who are female, nonwhite, or of non–European origin—boosts the team's innovative potential by providing critical insight into the needs and wants of overlooked or underserved end users.[110]

Marketing teams with just one Hispanic member, for example, are nearly twice as likely to understand—and effectively solve for—the problems inherent to convincing older Latinos to see a doctor about prostate trouble. R&D teams with just one native African member are, again, almost twice as likely to understand, and innovate products and services for, the millions of sub-Saharan consumers who grapple with limited access to reliable power and clean water. In case study after case study, in this new research we see that innate difference brings unique understand-

ing and vital insight to solving intractable problems, or to realizing unfulfilled market potential. At Morgan Stanley, one openly gay financial advisor spearheaded an accreditation campaign in domestic-partner estate planning that won the firm some $120 million in client assets because affluent members of the LGBT community preferred to work with financial advisors who understood their unique predicament. At Standard Chartered, one female executive (a native of India) drove the transformation of two bank branches in Kolkata and New Delhi into all-women branches, a move which drove up net sales at these bank branches by an impressive 127 percent and 75 percent, respectively, from 2009 to 2010. (This compared with a paltry 48 percent average among the bank's other ninety-plus Indian branches.)

Our findings underscore that there is a "diversity dividend": When companies and leaders know how to harness and leverage gender, generation, ethnicity, race, culture, and nationality there is a significant impact on the bottom line.

Innate difference is worth embracing for at least one other important reason: It can help win you a sponsor.[111] A sponsor is a leader who's committed to seeing you succeed and will go out on a limb to make sure you do. Sponsors are more powerful than mentors, because they're more vested in the outcome. They advocate for your next promotion, steer plum assignments your way, and protect you as you move up the learning curve because they see how their star will rise in conjunction with yours. When the research team at CTI probed "the sponsor effect" on multicultural professionals, we learned that not only are protégés of color more likely to be satisfied with their rate of advancement when they have a sponsor, but also that *sponsors* with protégés of color are more likely to be satisfied with their career progress (as compared to nonsponsors).

That is to say, it is precisely your difference that your superiors need to burnish their brand, build their team, extend their in-

novative capabilities, and ultimately succeed as leaders. It is your toolkit—the way you approach problems as a result of coming from a different background—that makes you worth sponsoring. It is your network, your access to clients or markets they might not otherwise be able to access that makes you valuable in growing their own networks. It is, finally, your insight into end users like yourself that gives them a competitive edge in the relentless competition to innovate. In this brave new world, the organization absolutely needs you to bring your whole self to work.

So don't downplay your difference. Commit to owning it.

# CONCLUSION

The first of three CTI research reports on EP was released in November 2012. Since that time I've given dozens of talks and led dozens of workshops on this subject matter. There have been many lessons learned. The following are particularly powerful.

**Ordinary mortals can crack the EP code.** These skills are eminently learnable. You don't have to be a born actor or be endowed with a James Earl Jones voice. I find it painful to remember how bad I was when I started doing public lectures. I used to stand behind large podiums reading from copious notes, determined that my audience hear every last piece of the evidence I had assembled to prove my point. I wince at the thought of how boring I must have been. Oftentimes I was also invisible. At five feet four (with heels) I could barely peer over the podium in many venues.

But I confronted my shortcomings and, by dint of hard work and with help from various coaches, lifted my game. Today I can command most spaces and stages. I have my own checklist: I prepare so thoroughly that the arc of my speech (vivid stories as well as pithy facts) gets beaten into my brain and I'm able to ditch my notes; I call ahead and ask that the podium be moved out of the way; and I use a lavaliere microphone so that I can roam free, making eye contact with as many people in the audience as possible. Over the years I've transformed my ability to engage and inspire an audience.

# Conclusion

If EP is learnable it's also doable. **You don't have to be some kind of genius** and ace all top picks across the three categories of gravitas, communication, and appearance. No need for straight A's. Not even Barack Obama is that good—and neither is Angelina Jolie. My advice here is to work with your strengths and try to nail three picks in each category. Take my approach to gravitas. My personality and skill sets position me well for number 1 (confidence), number 4 (emotional intelligence), and number 6 (vision). I have therefore sought to develop these natural strengths while making sure I don't totally mess up the other three picks. I also seek to avoid serious blunders.

**Figure out what is negotiable—and what is not.** In your drive to crack the EP code, don't compromise your authenticity to such an extent that it puts your soul in play. It will make you miserable and will also backfire, because in the end gravitas rests centrally on your true identity.

If you're a woman (or a gay person) working in a testosterone-laced organizational culture, don't put up with off-color or homophobic jokes. Make clear what your values are. If this means you're cut loose and encouraged to find employment elsewhere, so be it. Eventually your integrity and authenticity will win out.

Or if you're passionate about your field and yet work in an organization where coolness and restraint are admired behaviors, you may need to quit and find a work culture that values your enthusiasm and commitment. It's distressing to be constantly dialing back; it also eats into how much you can contribute to any venture.

A final word: **Commit to the work involved and embrace your EP journey.** It will be enormously empowering. Of course it will require a ton of energy. Learning how to command a room or read a client, figuring out how to use silence to punctuate a speech, finding the perfect skirt or suit to complement your body

170

type—none of this is easy and it will require hours of painstaking effort. But you can count on the results being transformative. Cracking the EP code will close the gap between merit and success, between where you are right now, and where you could be if you unleashed your full potential and allowed it to fly and soar. And it will make you feel quite wonderful.

Is a lack of executive presence holding you back from achieving your full potential? Take this assessment and find out.

1. You're making a presentation to twenty important people in your organization. Just before stepping into the meeting venue you receive a phone call from home which leaves you obviously infuriated. How do you handle this when you are expected to present immediately? Do you . . .

   a. Excuse yourself, delaying the meeting by ten or more minutes while you get yourself together
   b. Take a deep breath, walk into the meeting, and present with composure and professionalism, while exhibiting graceful gravitas
   c. Cancel the meeting because you are not in the mood and are angry

2. You are abroad, conducting a workshop in your area of expertise. Most of the participants are engaging and interactive as they have moderate to advanced experience in the area. This adds to the productivity of the workshop. However, there are one or two participants with little or no knowledge of the topic and who are not quite grasping some of the concepts you are introducing. As

a result, they interrupt you often by asking questions and/or requesting that you repeat yourself. Will you . . .

    a. Ignore their questions, hoping they will eventually stop interrupting you and catch up with the rest of the group

    b. Become annoyed and exhibit a "what do you want now" attitude

    c. Avoid the arrogant demeanor by offering a short break so that you can address the participants who do not seem to be catching on and find out where the breakdown of understanding/communication is

3. Your company is having a "Strategies Meeting" with management to address the direction the organization is going, as business has been slow and clients and customers have left. You know (as do others) that one of the main reasons this is happening is that the CEO is known to be curt, with old-fashioned ideas and/or concepts, and does not want to move in the direction of the present/future. He chooses you out of the group and asks your thoughts. Which exhibits gravitas?

    a. Taking a gulp of water and wiping your brow before speaking

    b. Standing up to speak with integrity, clarity, and confidence as you communicate your opinion/vision/thoughts with honesty and "truth to power"

    c. Asking if the CEO can ask someone else as you agree with his opinion

4. You are a director in a firm managing a team of twelve—both male and female. Your team has had the highest numbers in business development mainly due to two team members. The team member with the highest numbers is a woman of color, with a slight speech impairment and the second leader is a Cau-

casian male. The partners in the company want to promote someone by giving them a smaller team to lead and suggest that you choose wisely, indicating that the Caucasian male would be the better choice as his communication skills must be better. Which of the below would be the decision that exhibits emotional intelligence?

    a. You advocate for the woman of color with the speech impairment because she is clearly the better choice, as her performance measures twice the new business of the Caucasian male

    b. Tell the partners you are promoting the Caucasian male and tell the woman she just didn't cut it

    c. Ask the partners to make the decision for you because you'd rather not be put in that position

5. You are attending an all-day business convention with several speakers presenting throughout the day. You are asked (unexpectedly) to speak. After sitting and listening to what you considered boring speakers, you are tired and would rather leave than speak. In which scenario below does your body language communicate Executive Presence?

    a. You stand before your audience yawning, shoulders slumped, and begin to present while fidgeting throughout the presentation

    b. You decide to request a chair be put on the stage and commence to sit down and be comfortable during your presentation

    c. You have a glass of water just before you are announced and approach your audience with a welcoming smile, standing straight up and present with energy while engaging your audience throughout the presentation

6. As a team director, you must meet with your team and let them know that despite their hard drive to boost sales the second half of the quarter, executive management has decided that since the team consists of mostly women, it might be best to distribute them into other divisions. During the "team meeting," you communicate the news and state, "The reason this team is being split is because most of you are women." In your opinion which of the below is correct?

    a.  You handled this situation as a professional team leader, being truthful and direct

    b.  This is management's suggestion, and therefore, the team should not give any feedback on the situation

    c.  You exhibited one of the worst communication violations that detract from Executive Presence by making statements that reflect poor judgment and/or are gender biased

7. You are at a dinner reception honoring the leader of your organization. You are seated at a table with executives whom you do not know from other companies who are having various conversations amongst themselves. Which of the below is a good way to open conversation and show Executive Presence at the same time?

    a.  Initiate an off-the-cuff and off-the-record, casual conversation to break the ice

    b.  Begin coughing loudly to make your presence known and direct attention to yourself

    c.  Sit quietly and wait for someone to engage you in conversation

8. Janice has always held an excellent productivity record that has been recognized by her superiors as she is in the running for a promotion to vice president. Janice must speak to the

panel of superiors on her performance and vision if awarded the promotion. However, she is a bit concerned about the offer because the role requires her to do public and group speaking events. Janice is shy and not confident: her voice is low and quivers from nervousness when she speaks. Which of the below would Janice need to do to grasp the attention of her superiors and overcome her insecurity while exemplifying Executive Presence?

  a. Not worry about it because her performance speaks for itself. After all, it got her noticed for the promotion nomination

  b. Be assertive when speaking in front of the panel as they will find her grace and substance an added quality for the promotion

  c. Decline the nomination

9. You are quite excited because you have finally been invited to the golf outing this year. You are so excited about it that you decide to go shopping for new golf outfit. Once in the store, you find so many different types of outfits that you buy and pack three. Upon arrival, you realize that all the heavy hitters are there and you are the only female. Which outfit do you wear, as you want to be seen as another one of them and not just "the only woman there"?

  a. The attractive and short outfit with the flirty golf skirt that doesn't make your thighs look too big

  b. The authentic and appropriate golf shirt which brings attention to what you might have to say or even your golf score instead of the outfit

  c. Wear the outfit in option "B" but also choose a trendy pair of wedge-heeled sneakers. Have to have fashion in there somewhere!

10. Which of the below statements do you believe are true of Executive Presence?
   a. To look like a leader you must be perfect in all areas and slim
   b. Appearance is superficial nonsense that only superficial folks tune into
   c. More than anything, how we look translates into respect—for ourselves, for others, and for the work we are tasked to do

Total Your Score: 1. a-2, b-3, c-1; 2. a-2, b-1, c-3; 3. a-2, b-3, c-1; 4. a-3, b-2, c-1; 5. a-1, b-2, c-3; 6. a-3, b-2, c-1; 7. a-3, b-1, c-2; 8. a-2, b-3, c-1; 9. a-1, b-3, c-2; 10. a-1, b-2, c-3

| Your score | What it means |
|---|---|
| Less than 23 | Poor to fair. But don't worry, EP can be learned! Utilize mentors, sponsors, role models, and pointers in this book to burnish how you act, how you speak, and how you talk. |
| 24–26 | Good. You're on the right track! To bolster your EP, use coaches and other external resources to get a more solid grasp of all three pillars (gravitas, communication, and appearance). |
| 27–30 | Excellent. You've nailed EP! You have what it takes to convert your abilities into impact, influence, and results. |

For a more in-depth diagnostic of your or your colleagues' executive presence, please visit talentinnovation.org.

# INDEX OF EXHIBITS

# NOTES

1. Identities have been disguised.

2. Chia-Jung Tsay, "Sight over Sound in the Judgment of Music Performance," *Proceedings of the National Academy of Sciences in the United States of America* 110, no. 36 (2013): 14580–85, published online before print, August 19, 2013.

3. ABC News, "Top BP Executive Bob Dudley on 'Top Kill' Failure," interview on *This Week with George Stephanopoulos*, uploaded May 30, 2010, http://www.youtube.com/watch?v=kup3nTBo_-A&list=PLC8BBAB0172164E53&index=117.

4. *PBS NewsHour*, "'America Speaks to BP' Full Transcript: Bob Dudley Interview," air date July 1, 2010, http://www.pbs.org/newshour/bb/environment/july-dec10/dudleyfull_07-01.html.

5. The War in Afghanistan began on October 7, 2001, when the armed forces of the United States, the United Kingdom, Australia, France, and the Afghan United Front (Northern Alliance) launched Operation Enduring Freedom. See http://www.washingtonpost.com/wp-srv/nation/specials/attacked/transcripts/bushaddress_100801.htm.

6. Jack Welch and Suzy Welch, "J.P. Morgan: Jamie Dimon and the Horse He Fell Off," *Fortune*, May 24, 2012, http://management.fortune.cnn.com/2012/05/24/j-p-morgan-jamie-dimon-and-the-horse-he-fell-off/.

7. "Worst Moments of My Life: Pilot Tells of Ditching in Hudson," *Sydney Morning Herald*, February 6, 2009, http://www.smh.com.au/news/world/audio-reveals-exactly-what-happened--a-hrefhttpmediasmhcomaurid45888 blistenba/2009/02/06/1233423442580.html.

8. Tim Webb, "BP Boss Admits Job on the Line over Gulf Oil Spill," *Guardian*, May 13, 2010, http://www.theguardian.com/business/2010/may/13/bp-boss-admits-mistakes-gulf-oil-spill.

9. Stanley Reed, "Tony Hayward Gets His Life Back," *New York Times*, September 1, 2012, http://www.nytimes.com/2012/09/02/business/tony-hayward-former-bp-chief-returns-to-oil.html?pagewanted=all.

10. Claire Cain Miller and Catherine Rampell, "Yahoo Orders Home Workers Back to the Office," *New York Times*, February 25, 1013, http://www.nytimes.com/2013/02/26/technology/yahoo-orders-home-workers-back-to-the-office.html?pagewanted=all.

11. Kara Swisher, "'Physically Together': Here's the Internal Yahoo No-Work-From-Home Memo for Remote Workers and Maybe More," All Things D blog, February 22, 2013, http://allthingsd.com/20130222/physically-together-heres-the-internal-yahoo-no-work-from-home-memo-which-extends-beyond-remote-workers/.

12. Richard Branson, "Give People the Freedom of Where to Work," blog, February 25, 2013, http://www.virgin.com/richard-branson/give-people-the-freedom-of-where-to-work.

13. Charles Wallace, "Keep Taking the Testosterone," *Financial Times*, February 9, 2012, http://www.ft.com/intl/cms/s/0/68015bb2-51b8-11e1-a99d-00144feabdc0.html#axzz2NG4LUhfT.

14. Cenegenics website, http://www.cenegenics-nyc.com/mens -age-management-new-york-city.

15. Cindy Perman, "Wall Street's Secret Weapon for Getting an Edge," CNBC, July 11, 2012, http://www.cnbc.com /id/48149955.

16. Mayo Clinic website, "Testosterone Therapy: Key to Male Vitality?," http://www.mayoclinic.com/health/testosterone-therapy/MC00030/NSECTIONGROUP=2, accessed October 4, 2013.

17. Massimo Calabrisi, "Governor Christie on Sandy, Romney and Obama," *Time*, October 30, 2012, http://swampland.time .com/2012/10/30/gov-christie-on-sandy-romney-and-obama/.

18. Kate Zernike, "One Result of Hurricane: Bipartisanship Flows," *New York Times*, October 31, 2012, http://www .nytimes.com/2012/11/01/nyregion/in-stunning-about-face -chris-christie-heaps-praise-on-obama.html.

19. Burgess Everett, "Chris Christie on Hurricane Sandy: Hold-outs Are 'Stupid and Selfish,'" *Politico*, October 29, 2012, http://www.politico.com/news/stories/1012/83007.html.

20. "Chris Christie Criticizes Obama for 'Posing and Preening' as President," *Star-Ledger*, May 20, 2012, http://www .huffingtonpost.com/2012/05/20/chris-christie-obama_n _1531471.html; http://www.nj.com/news/index.ssf/2012/05 /gov_christie_obama_is_posing_a.html.

21. Christina Rexrode, "Struggling Bank of America Shakes Up Exec Ranks," AP on Yahoo, September 7, 2011, http:// news.yahoo.com/struggling-bank-america-shakes-exec -ranks-225348682.html; Halah Touryalai, "Bank of America's Latest Peril: Losing Merrill Lynch?," *Forbes* blog, September 2, 2013, http://www.forbes.com/sites/halah touryalai/2011/09/02/bank-of-americas-latest-peril-losing -merrill-lynch/.

22. Daniel Goleman, *Emotional Intelligence* (New York: Bantam Books, 1995).

23. Kara Swisher, "Survey Says: Despite Yahoo Ban, Most Tech Companies Support Work-from-Home for Employees," All Things D blog, February 25, 2013, http://allthingsd .com/20130225/survey-says-despite-yahoo-ban-most-tech -companies-support-work-from-home-for-employees/.

24. Robin J. Ely and Debra E. Meyerson, "An Organizational Approach to Undoing Gender: The Unlikely Case of Offshore Oil Platforms," *Research in Organizational Behavior* 30 (2010): 3–34.

25. Andrea Tantaros, "Material Girl Michelle Obama Is a Modern-Day Marie Antoinette on a Glitzy Spanish Vacation," editorial, *Daily News*, August 5, 2010, http://www .nydailynews.com/opinion/material-girl-michelle-obama -modern-day-marie-antoinette-glitzy-spanish-vacation -article-1.200134?pgno=1.

26. See, for example, Shawna Thomas, "Michelle Obama: 'Hadiya Pendleton Was Me and I Was Her,'" NBC News, April 10, 2013, http://firstread.nbcnews.com /_news/2013/04/10/17692560-michelle-obama-hadiya -pendleton-was-me-and-i-was-her?lite.

27. "Angelina Jolie Fact Sheet," UNHCR, http://www.unhcr.org /pages/49db77906.html, accessed October 4, 2013.

28. Walter Isaacson, *Steve Jobs* (New York: Simon & Schuster, 2011), 363.

29. Sheryl Sandberg, *Lean In: Women, Work, and the Will to Lead* (New York: Knopf, 2013), 3, 17, 167.

30. Steve Fishman, "Al Gore's Golden Years," *New York*, May 5, 2013, http://nymag.com/news/features/al-gore-2013-5/.

31. The study, conducted by Quantified Impressions, analyzed financial executives' communication effectiveness by apply-

ing a suite of software tools developed in conjunction with the Kellogg School of Management at Northwestern University and enlisting a panel of experts along with one thousand listeners to augment the digital analysis. The most effective financial spokesperson turned out to be Richard Davis, CEO of US Bancorp, because he appeared "genuine, emotionally connected to his audience, and relaxed in front of the camera," according to Quantified's president, Noah Zandan. http://www.quantifiedimpressions.com/blog/quantified -impressions-new-scientific-analysis-of-top-financial-communicators-pinpoints-how-speakers-build-trust-influence-audiences/.

32. Quantified Impressions study.

33. Cited by Sue Shellenbarger in "Is This How You Really Talk?," *Wall Street Journal*, April 23, 2013, http://online.wsj .com/article/SB10001424127887323735604578440851083674898.html.

34. Charles Moore, "The Invincible Mrs. Thatcher," *Vanity Fair*, December 2011, http://www.vanityfair.com/politics /features/2011/12/margaret-thatcher-201112.

35. David Baker, "Hollywood Vocal Coach Helped Margaret Thatcher Lose Her 'Shrill Tones,'" *Mail Online*, February 5, 2012, http://www.dailymail.co.uk/news/article-2096785 /Hollywood-vocal-coach-helped-Margaret-Thatcher-lose -shrill-tones.html; Moore, "The Invincible Mrs. Thatcher."

36. William J. Mayew, Christopher A. Parsons, and Mohan Venkatachalam, "Voice Pitch and the Labor Market Success of Male Chief Executive Officers," *Evolution and Human Behavior* 34 (2013): 243–48.

37. Melissa Korn, "What Does a Successful CEO Sound Like? Try a Deep Bass," *Wall Street Journal*, April 18, 2013, http:// blogs.wsj.com/atwork/2013/04/18/what-does-a-successful

-ceo-sound-like-try-a-deep-bass/?blog_id=226&post
_id=882&mod=wsj_valettop_email.

38.  "Americans Speak Out, Select the 'Best and Worst Voices in
     America' in Online Polling by the Center for Voice Disorders
     of Wake Forest University," press release, Wake Forest Uni-
     versity Baptist Medical Center, September 10, 2001, http://
     www.nrcdxas.org/articles/voices.html.

39.  William J. Mayew and Mohan Venkatachalam, "Voice Pitch
     and the Labor Market Success of Male Chief Executive Of-
     ficers," Sidney Winter Lecture Series, April 12, 2013, http://
     tippie.uiowa.edu/accounting/mcgladrey/winterpapers/mpv
     _ehb_accepted%20-%20mayew.pdf.

40.  Sue Shellenbarger, "Is This How You Really Talk?,"
     *Wall Street Journal*, April 23, 2013, http://online.wsj.com
     /article/SB10001424127887323735604578440851083674
     4898.html.

41.  Huffingtonpost.com audience measurement, Quantcast,
     http://www.quantcast.com/huffingtonpost.com, accessed
     April 4, 2013.

42.  Erik Hedegaard, "Beauty and the Blog: *Rolling Stone*'s 2006
     Feature on Arianna Huffington," *Rolling Stone*, December
     14, 2006, http://www.rollingstone.com/culture/news/beauty
     -and-the-blog-rolling-stones-2006-feature-on-arianna
     -huffington-20110207#ixzz2gIpcBwfa.

43.  Allen Dodds Frank, "Former Wall Street Executive Sal-
     lie Krawcheck Critiques Financial Reform Policy," *Daily
     Beast*, October 16, 2012, http://www.thedailybeast.com
     /articles/2012/10/16/former-wall-street-executive-sallie
     -krawcheck-critiques-financial-reform-policy.html.

44.  Carol Kinsey Goman, "The Body Language Win-
     ner of the Third Presidential Debate," *Forbes*, Octo-
     ber 23, 2013, http://www.forbes.com/sites/carolkinsey

goman/2012/10/23/the-body-language-winner-of-the -third-presidential-debate/.

45. When only first names are used they are pseudonyms. Identifying details have been changed to protect confidentiality.

46. See Amy Cuddy's TED talk at http://www.ted.com/talks /amy_cuddy_your_body_language_shapes_who_you_are .html, posted October 2012.

47. Kate Murphy, "The Right Stance Can Be Reassuring," *New York Times*, May 3, 2013, http://www .nytimes.com/2013/05/05/fashion/the-right-stance-can-be -reassuring-studied.html?emc=eta1&_r=0.

48. Elise Hu, "Campaign Trail Tears: The Changing Politics of Crying," NPR, November 25, 2011, http://www .npr.org/2011/11/25/142599676/campaign-trail-tears-the -changing-politics-of-crying.

49. *Saturday Night Live*, "Democratic Debate '88," transcript from Season 13, Episode 10, available at http://snltranscripts .jt.org/87/87jdemocrats.phtml.

50. Nancy Benac, "Has the Political Risk of Emotion, Tears Faded?," *USA Today*, December 19, 2007, http://usatoday30 .usatoday.com/news/politics/election2008/2007-12-19 -emotion-politics_N.htm.

51. Patrick Sawer, "How Maggie Thatcher Was Remade," *Telegraph*, January 8, 2012, http://www.telegraph.co.uk /news/politics/margaret-thatcher/8899746/How-Maggie -Thatcher-was-remade.html.

52. Photos reprinted with permission. http://www.plosone.org /article; Nancy L. Etcoff, Shannon Stock, Lauren E. Haley, Sarah A. Vickery, and David M. House, "Cosmetics as a Feature of the Extended Human Phenotype: Modulation of the Perception of Biologically Important Facial Signals," *PLoS*

*ONE* 6, no. 10 (2011): e25656, 2011, doi:10.1371/journal
.pone.0025656.

53. Etcoff et al., "Cosmetics as a Feature of the Extended Human Phenotype," 7.

54. Check out the Occupy Wall Street debate at the Oxford Union Society on YouTube: http://www.youtube.com/watch?v=CoWiV6Q8qME.

55. Deborah L. Rhode, *The Beauty Bias: The Injustice of Appearance in Life and Law* (New York: Oxford University Press, 2010).

56. Timothy Noah, "Chris Christie's Crowd-Sourced Weight Is . . . ," *New Republic*, September 30, 2011, http://www.newrepublic.com/blog/timothy-noah/95641/chris-christies-crowd-sourced-weight#.

57. John Kenney, "The Unbearable Lightness of Leading," *New York Times*, March 6, 2010: http://www.nytimes.com/2010/03/07/opinion/07kenney.html.

58. OPEN N.Y., "The Measure of a President," *New York Times*, October 6, 2008, http://www.nytimes.com/interactive/2008/10/06/opinion/06opchart.html?_r=0.

59. Leslie Kwoh, "Want to Be CEO? What's Your BMI?," *Wall Street Journal*, January 16, 2013, http://online.wsj.com/article/SB10001424127887324595704578241573341483946.html.

60. Rhode, *The Beauty Bias*, 21.

61. Ben Shapiro, *Project President: Bad Hair and Botox on the Road to the White House* (Nashville, TN: Thomas Nelson, 2007), 53.

62. Ibid., 54.

63. OPEN N.Y., "The Measure of a President."

64. Shapiro, *Project President*, 54.

65. "Diana Taylor Addresses Her and Bloomberg's Height Dif-

ference," *Huffington Post*, January 10, 2011, updated January 10, 2012, http://www.huffingtonpost.com/2011/01/10/diana-taylor-bloomberg-do_n_807031.html.

66. Chris Woolston, "A Costly Turf War," *Los Angeles Times*, January 29, 2012, http://articles.latimes.com/2012/jan/29/image/la-ig-balding-20120129.

67. American Society of Plastic Surgeons, "2012 Cosmetic Surgery Gender Distribution," 10, http://www.plasticsurgery.org/news-and-resources/2012-plastic-surgery-statistics.html.

68. "Brotox? Cosmetic Procedures Rise, Growing Number of Men Turn to Botox," *ABC Action News*, WXYZ, June 14, 2013, http://www.wxyz.com/dpp/news/brotox-cosmetic-procedures-rises-growing-number-of-men-turn-to-botox.

69. Melissa Preddy, "Quicktips: From Upper-Arm Tucks to Up-in-Arms Truckers," Reynolds Center, BusinessJournalism.org, April 30, 2013, http://businessjournalism.org/2013/04/30/quicktips-from-upper-arm-tucks-to-up-in-arms-truckers/.

70. William J. vanden Heuvel, "LETTERS: Another Look at F.D.R.," *New York Times*, January 12, 2010, http://query.nytimes.com/gst/fullpage.html?res=9C02E4DF1F30F931A25752C0A9669D8B63.

71. Ibid.

72. Margaret Thatcher, "Speech to Finchley Conservatives," January 31, 1976, Margaret Thatcher Foundation, http://www.margaretthatcher.org/document/102947.

73. Michael Cockerell, "How to Be a Tory Leader," *Telegraph*, December 1, 2005, http://www.telegraph.co.uk/culture/3648425/How-to-be-a-Tory-leader.html.

74. Mary Gottschalk, "Thatcher Improves Image with Pricey Styles," *Tulsa World*, March 12, 1989, http://www.tulsaworld.com/site/printerfriendlystory.aspx?articleid=14111.

75. Stephen Moss, "Looking for Maggie," *Guardian*, March 6, 2003, http://www.theguardian.com/books/2003/mar/07/biography.media.

76. Zach Johnson, "Olivia Wilde: I Was Told Actresses Should Never Audition in Short Skirts," *Us Weekly*, November 16, 2012, http://www.usmagazine.com/entertainment/news/olivia-wilde-i-was-told-actresses-should-never-audition-in-short-skirts-20121611#ixzz2gPjZXb5e.

77. Catalyst, "Catalyst Pyramid: U.S. Women in Business," New York: Catalyst, 2013.

78. "Jesse Jackson Slams Obama for 'Acting Like He's White' in Jena 6 Case," ABC News, September 19, 2007, http://abcnews.go.com/blogs/headlines/2007/09/jesse-jackson-s/.

79. Stanley Crouch, "What Obama Isn't: Black Like Me on Race," *New York Daily News*, November 2, 2006, http://www.nydailynews.com/Archives/Opinions/Obama-Isnt-Black-Race-Article-1.585922.

80. Sylvia Hewlett, Kerrie Peraino, Laura Sherbin, and Karen Sumberg, "The Sponsor Effect: Breaking Through the Last Glass Ceiling," *Harvard Business Review* Research Report, December 2010, 26.

81. Virginia E. Schein, "The Relationship Between Sex Role Stereotypes and Requisite Management Characteristics," *Journal of Applied Psychology* 57 (1973): 95–100; Virginia E. Schein, "The Relationship Between Sex Role Stereotypes and Requisite Management Characteristics Among Female Managers," *Journal of Applied Psychology* 60 (1975): 340–44; Virginia E. Schein, "Managerial Sex Typing: A Persistent and Pervasive Barrier to Women's Opportunities," in M. Davidson and R. Burke, eds., *Women in Management: Current Research Issues* (London: Paul Chapman, 1994).

82. "Women 'Take Care,' Men 'Take Charge': Stereotyping

of U.S. Business Leaders Exposed," Catalyst, 2005, http://
www.catalyst.org/knowledge/women-take-care-men-take
-charge-stereotyping-us-business-leaders-exposed.

83. See Veronica F. Nieva and Barbara A. Gutek, "Sex Effects on
Evaluation," *Academy of Management Review* 5, no. 2 (1980).

84. Peggy McIntosh, "White Privilege: Unpacking the Invisible
Knapsack," *Peace and Freedom*, July/August 1989.

85. "How Are Powerful Women Perceived," *Anderson Cooper
360*, CNN, March 12, 2013, http://www.cnn.com/video
/data/2.0/video/bestoftv/2013/03/13/ac-powerful-women
-experiment.cnn.html.

86. Madeline E. Heilman, Aaron S. Wallen, Daniella Fuchs, and
Melinda M. Tamkins, "Penalties for Success: Reactions to
Women Who Succeed at Male Gender-Typed Tasks," *Journal
of Applied Psychology* 89, no. 3 (2004): 416–27.

87. Kim M. Elsesser and Janet Lever, "Does Gender Bias Against
Female Leaders Persist? Quantitative and Qualitative Data
from a Large-Scale Survey," *Human Relations* 64, no. 12 (2011):
1555–78, http://hum.sagepub.com/content/64/12/1555.

88. Oliver Balch, "The Bachelet Factor: The Cultural Leg-
acy of Chile's First Female President," *Guardian*, December
13, 2009, http://www.guardian.co.uk/world/2009/dec/13
/michelle-bachelet-chile-president-legacy.

89. Ibid.

90. Katrin Bennhold, "Taking the Gender Fight Worldwide,"
*New York Times*, March 29, 2011, http://www.nytimes
.com/2011/03/30/world/europe/30iht-letter30.html?page
-wanted=2&ref=michellebachelet.

91. Patricia Sellers, "Facing Up to the Female Power Conundrum,"
CNN Money, January 31, 2011, http://postcards.blogs
.fortune.cnn.com/2011/01/31/facing-up-to-the-female
-power-conundrum/.

92. Jessica Valenti, "She Who Dies with the Most 'Likes' Wins?," *Nation*, November 29, 2012, http://www.thenation.com /blog/171520/she-who-dies-most-likes-wins.

93. Sandberg, *Lean In*, 40.

94. Catalyst, "The Double-Bind Dilemma for Women in Leadership: Damned If You Do, Doomed If You Don't," Catalyst, 2007, http://www.catalyst.org/knowledge/double-bind -dilemma-women-leadership-damned-if-you-do-doomed-if -you-dont-0.

95. David Mattingly, "Michelle Obama Likely Target of Conservative Attacks," CNN Politics.com, June 12, 2008, http://www.cnn.com/2008/POLITICS/06/12/michelle. obama/.

96. Jeremy Holden, "Fox News' E. D. Hill Teased Discussion of Obama Dap: 'A Fist Bump? A Pound? A Terrorist Fist Jab?,'" June 6, 2008, cited on Media Matters for America, http://mediamatters.org/video/2008/06/06/fox-news-ed -hill-teased-discussion-of-obama-dap/143674.

97. Avery Stone, "What If Paula Deen Had Called Someone a Fag?," HuffPost Blog, July 1, 2013, http://www .huffingtonpost.com/avery-stone/what-if-paula-deen-had -called-someone-a-fag_b_3526186.html.

98. "Ireland Baldwin Talks About Father Alec Baldwin's Infamous 'Pig' Voicemail," *Huffington Post*, September 6, 2012, http://www.huffingtonpost.com/2012/09/06/ireland -baldwin-alec-baldwin-pig-call_n_1861892.html.

99. Diane Johnson, "Christine Lagarde: Changing of the Guard," *Vogue*, September 2011, 706, http://www.vogue.com /magazine/article/christine-lagarde-changing-of-the- guard/#1.

100. Ibid.

101. Richard Branson, "Richard Branson on Taking Risks,"

*Entrepreneur*, June 10, 2013, http://www.entrepreneur.com
/article/226942.

102. Eleanor Clift, "Kirsten Gillibrand's Moment: Women's
Champion vs. Military Assaults," *Daily Beast*, May 10, 2013,
http://www.thedailybeast.com/articles/2013/05/10/kirsten
-gillibrand-s-moment-women-s-champion-vs-military
-assaults.html.

103. Steve Williams, "Elizabeth Warren: It Gets Better," Care2,
January 27, 2012, http://www.care2.com/causes/elizabeth
-warren-it-gets-better-video.html.

104. Sanford Levinson, "Identifying the Jewish Lawyer: Reflec-
tions on the Construction of Professional Identity," *Cardozo
Law Review* 14, no. 1577 (1993): 1578–79. Interestingly,
Levinson also used the multilingual metaphor to describe his
spheres of identity as a Jewish lawyer.

105. Sylvia Ann Hewlett, Carolyn Buck Luce, Cornel West,
Helen Chernikoff, Danielle Samalin, and Peggy Shiller, *Invisible Lives: Celebrating and Leveraging Diversity Talent in
the Executive Suite* (New York: Center for Work-Life Policy,
2005). The Center for Work-Life Policy changed its name to
the Center for Talent Innovation in 2012.

106. Ibid.

107. Sylvia Ann Hewlett and Karen Sumberg, *The Power of "Out":
LGBT in the Workplace* (New York: Center for Work-Life Policy, 2011).

108. Sylvia Ann Hewlett and Ripa Rashid, *Winning the War for
Talent in Emerging Markets: Why Women Are the Solution* (Boston, Mass.: Harvard Business Review Press, 2011).

109. Sylvia Hewlett, Melinda Marshall, and Laura Sherbin, with
Tara Gonsalves, *Innovation, Diversity, and Market Growth*
(New York: Center for Talent Innovation, 2013); Sylvia
Ann Hewlett, Melinda Marshall, and Laura Sherbin, "How

# Notes

Diversity Can Drive Innovation," *Harvard Business Review*, December 2013.

110. Ibid.

111. See Sylvia Ann Hewlett, *Forget a Mentor, Find a Sponsor: The New Way to Fast-Track Your Career* (Boston, Mass.: Harvard Business Review Press, 2013).

# INDEX

Page *numbers of illustrations appear in italics.*

# Index

# Index

Deloitte Consulting, 60–61, 69, 111, 159

Digby, Suzi, 52, 55, 56, 120, 133–34

Dimon, Jamie, 19

dot-com bubble, 17

Dougan, Brady, 59–60, 71

Dudley, Bob, 11, 15, 25

DuHaime, Mike, 26

Dukakis, Michael, 93, 94

Duke University

Fuqua School of Business, 53

research on timbre and pitch, 53

Dunn, Brian, 38

Ebbers, Bernard, 19

Elam, Deb, 40, 69, 89

Ellison, Larry, 38

emotional intelligence (EQ), 15, 27–31

ability to read a room and, 65

assertiveness and, 63

developing, 31

Marissa Mayer lacking, 28–29

Michelle Obama and, 31

oil rig example, 29

"reading a room" and, 30

Romney lacking, 27–28

trust-building and, 30

Enron, 17

Equality and Human Rights Commission (EHRC), 147

Erni, Anne, 18, 76

Etcoff, Nancy, 83–84

executive coach, 117–18

Executive Presence (EP). *See also* appearance; communication; gravitas

appearance and, 7–9

assertiveness as core trait, 61

authenticity and, 170

author's loss of, xviii–xx

author's rebuilding of, xx–xxi

Bob Dudley and, 12

body language and posture, importance of, 69

commitment to, 170–71

contestants in musical competition and, 2–4

core characteristics, 81

cracking the EP code, 5–10

CTI research reports on, 169

decisiveness and, 23

The Fine Line of Executive Presence (Figure 10), *132*

fragility of, xviii

"grace under fire" and, 6, 17, 18–21

gravitas as the core characteristic, 5–6, 16

leadership and, 1

minorities and, 147–67

as precondition for success, 2

projecting confidence and, 6

skills as doable, 170

skills as learnable, 169

telegraphing your image, 1–2

three pillars of, 5, *6*

traits that confer EP, 49, 184n31

who has it, 1

# Index

# Index

# Index

# Index

# Index

Sylvia Ann Hewlett is an economist and the founder and CEO of the Center for Talent Innovation, a Manhattan-based think tank where she chairs the Task Force for Talent Innovation, a group of eighty global companies focused on fully realizing the new streams of labor in the global marketplace. She is the co-director of the Women's Leadership Program at the Columbia Business School.